T4-APV-139

THE GOALS OF
HUMAN SEXUALITY

Irving Singer

THE GOALS OF HUMAN SEXUALITY

SCHOCKEN BOOKS • NEW YORK

Contents

Preface

Until recently—within the last ten years perhaps—there were various questions about human sexuality that could hardly be discussed even in medical treatises. The nature of the orgasm, in both male and female, is one of these questions. Many people, women in particular, have always refused to believe that anyone could properly analyze the female orgasm. In her novel *The Golden Notebook*, Doris Lessing has one of her characters describe a lecture given by a distinguished physician to the medical staff of a London hospital. As soon as he begins to talk about the female orgasm, all the women doctors walk out. They are certain that a man could not speak on this topic with any understanding. The woman to whom the character recounts the anecdote obviously feels the same way. She is particularly scornful of authorities who pretend to prove the impossibility of what she calls her "vaginal orgasm":

> "Do you know that there are eminent physiologists who say women have no physical basis for vaginal orgasm?"
> "Then they don't know much, do they?" [1]

In the decade that has passed since Miss Lessing's novel appeared, new work has been done in this field—by women investigators as well as men. It has also become a topic that ordinary people are able to discuss more freely than ever before. The nature of the orgasm is worth studying because it reveals some of the major goals of human sexuality. The goals of sexuality are not all alike, however, and we need not assume in advance that the orgasm is always the same either as a physiological process or as a psychological event. In fact, as I shall suggest, there is considerable reason to believe in a diversity of types of orgasm that women undergo.

In relation to questions about "clitoral" versus "vaginal" orgasms, most sexologists are convinced either that there is no fundamental difference between them, or else that one kind is healthy or normal and the other is not. As opposed to these alternatives, I shall argue for a third possibility: namely, that there are important differences between responses which have been considered clitoral or vaginal, and that in principle each is as normal or healthy as the other. And though the male's orgasmic experience is not a mirror image of the female's, there too we shall find a variety of responses each of which may be optimal for certain people under certain circumstances.

In speculating about the diversity of sexual response, I employ a pluralistic approach which William James continually recommended in his attempts to analyze human experience in general. He used it most effectively in *The Varieties of Religious Experience*, a book that virtually created the scientific study of religious phenomenology. At each point James denied that everything which might authentically be called a religious experience belonged to a uniform pattern or could be subsumed under a single model of explanation. He also denied that religious attitudes could be reduced to the sexual. In our age sexual experience has acquired the pervasive importance which religion had at the time that James was writing. And one might even say that for many people nowadays sexuality offers the only equivalent to religious ecstasy that has any meaning in the contemporary world. It therefore becomes imperative that sexual experience should not itself be reduced to constraining categories or unitary models of what is natural or normal or uniquely desirable.

As a way of arguing for the pluralistic character of erotic response, I shall distinguish between different modes of sexual phenomenology which I call the "sensuous" and the "passionate," different sociological patterns of behavior which Kinsey refers to as the "two systems of sexual mores," and in general different attitudes that contribute to the variegated ways in which human beings attain sexual release. Within this great diversity one must also find room for inhibitions that may be salutary as well as unavoidable. Not every instance of "Victorian" or "Puritanical" restraint is harmful or merely an unfortunate residue of childhood training. What is called repression is sometimes the result of innate tendencies which are as much a part of sexuality as "liberated" inclinations characterized by a lack of inhibitions. In treating inhibitions as a natural force, this book owes much to the work of recent ethologists. They have described many instances in which animals are, as it were, "programmed" with inhibitory reactions that deflect them from behavior detrimental to the survival of the species. In the case of human beings, however, sexual inhibitions are more complex: they are subject to greater social influence and are less constant in their operation—fading in and out in ways that are often erratic.

Some of these human inhibitions may be related to the dynamics of reproduction. In the Appendix, several problems in reproductive physiology are discussed with this possibility in mind. Though the Appendix is more technical than the other chapters, the general reader may find it useful as an introduction to unresolved questions about sexuality to which the theories of this book can be applied.

There are two purposes that the book as a whole tries to fulfill: first, to delineate the different and possibly irreducible forms of sexual response that exist in different men and women on different occasions, or at different times in a person's life; and second, to suggest that people may be less alike in their sexual responsiveness than most recent sexologists have led us to believe. One contemporary attitude towards sex is exemplified by the health food enthusiast whom *Time* magazine quotes as saying: "If I eat yang I slip into my desire body. Yin food makes me more ethereal. Women often find what is soft and gentle in a man most appealing about him. It's much easier to be tender on a yin diet." [2] In this book we shall not be discussing the relationship between sex and diet, but we shall try to understand why it is that some people favor their "desire body," others cultivate the tenderness of their yin, and still others seek to harmonize the two. Some women do admire "what is soft and gentle in a man," but some prefer the vigorous and aggressive male. We must not assume that there is an essentially "right" or "correct" sexual response, or any one way which will work for all persons on all occasions. Since the goals of human sexuality are multiple, we need to discover the many ways in which they can be achieved with joy and even dignity.

This book was completed with the help of a grant from the Rockefeller Foundation. Chapter 3 and the Appendix were written in collaboration with my wife, Josephine Singer, who worked with me on the rest of the book as well. I would like to express my gratitude to her, to the officers of the Rockefeller Foundation, to colleagues who have read chapters of the manuscript, and to several friends who encouraged me with their good wishes in this endeavor and above all with their honest criticism. I am also indebted to my editors, George P. Brockway of Norton and Sir Alan S. Parkes, for their expert assistance with various parts of the text. I am particularly grateful to those men and women whose personal reports about their sexual behavior are included in the book. Without their testimony, it could never have advanced beyond the level of mere speculation.

I.S.

THE GOALS OF
HUMAN SEXUALITY

Introduction

THE NEW SEXOLOGY

The erotic life has been a subject of western thought ever since Plato spoke about that universal drive called eros which caused all creatures to seek for completion in another member of their species. But the scientific study of sex is fairly recent in its origins. There are some who trace the beginnings of sexology to the writings of Krafft-Ebing and Havelock Ellis at the end of the nineteenth century; others may want to go as far back as Leeuwenhoek in the seventeenth century, or even to Leonardo da Vinci in the fifteenth. In many ways, however, the science of sexology begins with the more theoretical generalizations about sexual behavior which Freud articulated in his *Three Essays on the Theory of Sexuality*, written in 1905 and revised in subsequent years.[1] Freud incorporates a long tradition of medical presuppositions about sex, some of them originating with the Greeks; and in certain respects contemporary sexology has made the advances it can claim by emancipating itself from the influence of both Freud and his predecessors. Freud himself lamented the fact that so little had been done to verify or falsify by empirical means those generalizations about sex which had been handed down from one authority to another. He wished to turn all speculation about such matters into purely scientific investigations; the possibility that psychoanalysis itself would someday become a science comparable to physics or chemistry underlay many of his own hypotheses.

Beginning with the successors to Freud, particularly those who criticized him for being too speculative, sexology began to emulate the quantitative and empirical methodology of the well-established sciences. Sociologists like Kinsey approached sexual phenomena with the same concern for statistical accuracy that Kinsey himself had revealed in studying the behavior of gall wasps. And in the work of Masters and Johnson, human sexuality became a subject for laboratory research comparable to what many scientists were doing in their experiments with the physiology of reproduction among lower animals. Although the enterprise is still very recent, and frequently impeded by distrust towards anyone who seeks the truth in these areas, sexology may now pride itself on being at least quasi-scientific in its primitive beginnings.

But having freed itself from many vagaries of the past, sexology faces dangers which are characteristic of the life sciences in general. In attempting to be quantitative and precise, it easily becomes alienated from that human reality which the earlier tradition— with its roots in literature and the humanism of classical studies —reflected as a matter of course. People under investigation, whether they are being questioned by a sociologist or observed by a physiologist, do not always reveal what is most important about themselves, and those who submit to observation are often unrepresentative of those who do not. However intuitive they may have been, the writings of poets, novelists, historians, and even philosophers frequently described the varieties of human affect with greater insight than can be attained through scientific research.

The new sexology to which this book addresses itself may eventually succeed in combining the precision of science with this greater sensitivity to human differences which often appears in the humanistic tradition. One cannot hope to understand the goals of sexuality if one limits oneself to either of these alternatives. Without the methods of scientific investigation, the humanities founder in loose generalizations, which may easily turn into dogmatic beliefs showing none of that sensitivity to which I referred. Without the immersion in everyday reality which the humanities take as their province, the life sciences lose their relevance to life itself and often blur the differences between individual responses.

It is this kind of blurring which has hampered each of the earlier stages in sexological theory. Both Freud and Masters and Johnson suffer from an essentialism which underlies most of their analyses. In the case of Freud, this essentialism—by which I mean the assumption that in all sexological matters there must be a single, basic, uniform pattern ordained by nature itself—derives from the doctrine of the libido which I shall be discussing in the following section. Masters and Johnson too believe in uniformities which serve as a normative basis for their therapeutic advice as well as their generalizations about sexual response. Though Freud emphasizes the differences between male and female, whereas Masters and Johnson emphasize the similarities, they both think of sexuality as a specific entity more or less alike in all human beings. Moreover, Masters and Johnson resemble Freud in assuming that within this uniformity each of the sexes must have its own basic pattern: one for the male and one for the female. As a consequence, they employ essentialistic criteria for the normality and preferability of one or another type of sexual response. To this extent, Masters and Johnson are traditionalists no less than Freud and the Freudians whom they criticize. Both show the influences of a doctrinaire philosophy—its origins in Plato and Aristotle—which believed that there must be a single structure to all sexuality and that it expresses itself in appropriate responses of male and female.

Much of this book will devote itself to a pluralistic approach that seeks to retain the scientific orientation of sexologists like Masters and Johnson while also avoiding their essentialism. By "pluralism" I mean the refusal to assume in advance that nature prescribes a unitary model for male and female response, that there is any one norm which could indicate how all men or women must behave in order to function properly, that there is a unique mode of consummation that satisfies male or female sexuality, that there is a universal condition which constitutes or structures sexual response in all people on all occasions, or that there is a single instinct or biologic system basic to human sexuality.

The sexologist who best combines a scientific attitude with some appreciation of the pluralistic approach is Kinsey. But even he often shows signs of essentialism, as in passages such as the following:

> Apparently many females, even though they may be slow to respond in coitus, may masturbate to orgasm in a matter of a minute or two. Masturbation thus appears to be a better test than coitus of the female's actual capacities; and there seems to be something in the coital technique which is responsible for her slower responses there.[2]

The first sentence in this passage states an empirical generalization that is undoubtedly true: many women achieve orgasm through masturbation more quickly than in coitus. From this, Kinsey concludes that masturbation indicates "the female's actual capacities" better than coitus. To say this, however, is to assume that all orgasms are alike and therefore sexual capacity can be measured regardless of how they are induced. It also assumes that a woman's capacities can be gauged by the speed with which she reaches orgasm rather than the degree and quality of her sexual enjoyment or in general her response to intimacy with some particular man. And finally, it assumes that there is something that may be called the female's capacity—not merely in the sense of summing up the empirical data about an individual woman, but rather as a clue to what *all* women must be like in their sexual nature.

It is this kind of essentialism, this fundamental belief that science can disclose an essence of human sexuality, which needs to be exorcised from the new science of sexology. The essentialism of Masters and Johnson will preoccupy much of our subsequent discussion, but essentialism in Freud's doctrine of the libido is worth considering here. Those who criticize a great man, either directly or indirectly, often appropriate some of his basic assumptions about the nature of their joint investigation. It is the link that facilitates communication and thereby enables the critics to develop a position of their own. This has happened in relation to Freud. By studying his essentialism, as well as a corresponding essentialism in his critics, we may be able to take a new direction that will free us from both.

If Freud had been writing at the time of Plato, he would have called his doctrine of the libido a poetic "myth." The myth of the libido suggests that the erotic in man can be explained by reference to two separate coordinates: one is society or civilization, and that is highly variable; but the other is a fixed and determinate instinct, a source of energy basically similar for all human beings. This source of energy Freud called the libido. Though he could not observe it in isolation, he felt that it had to be posited as an innate force throughout sexual development. Since the libido recognizes no imperative other than immediate satisfaction, it had to be controlled by the restraints of society. Such controls insinuate themselves into the unconscious, but in principle they are external to the libido itself. Society is therefore inherently repressive, and so permanently at war with the sexual instinct.

Now why do I call this a myth? Surely we all realize that we have sexual impulses that society restrains; and in the polymorphous hedonism of infancy we may envisage the freedom to enjoy organic pleasures that life in society eventually destroys. One might say that in the infant the libido shows itself forth, and that later developments reveal its vicissitudes within an alien dimension. This, however, is not Freud's argument. The libido is not limited to the observable behavior of the infant or, for that matter, of anyone else. The libido is a hypothetical construct, something that underlies all human sexuality but never can be observed in itself. Furthermore, it changes inwardly as the individual matures. From the polymorphous perverse condition of infancy, it moves through a series of transformations that eventuate in what Freud calls normal genitality. At all stages in its development, the libido appears only in its interaction with society. It always remains hidden, but it alone provides man with a sexual nature that society may then modify and control. The myth is fascinating, but if man does not have "a nature"—a single, uniform, and universal being—it is quite misleading.

To say that man has a nature, that he has an underlying libido, that he is programmed by an integral and ultimately unified instinct of sexuality, is to say that his development has a fixed direction and can be plotted in advance of any individual's experience. *Normal* development would thus involve progress in growth or maturation which is determined by the organic impulse itself. We speak that way about processes such as walking or even talking. It is as if the legs were "made" for walking. Children whose bone structure or bodily coordination prevents them from walking, instead of enabling them to, are deficient in a way that we all recognize. If sexuality is comparable, as Freud believes, then it must lead to a process that would be analogous in its uniformity to the process of walking. He thought that for sexuality this process, the relevant expression of the instinct, must be coital behavior related to the needs of reproduction. In its normal, i.e., normative and not just statistically frequent, employment, the sexual instinct had to eventuate in heterosexual coitus. Man's inherent sexuality would thus consist in the stages of the libido, which change as an individual matures but always in the direction of a single goal. For Freud this process is essentially the same as in the development "of a caterpillar into a butterfly. The turning-point of this development is the subordination of all the component sexual instincts under the primacy of the genitals and along with this the subjection of sexuality to the reproductive function." [3] We thus become fully sexual, normal and mature in the only way that applies to human nature, when we outgrow the caterpillar stage of libidinal development and direct our erotic interests towards the genital behavior of coitus. Sexual perversions deflect the libido from its natural progression. They freeze it into one or another of its preliminary stages. Neuroses do not arrest the libido, but they too interfere with its normal functioning. In neither perversion nor neurosis can the libido reach the definitive satisfaction, the appropriate release of tension, prescribed by the sheer genetic structure of every human organism.

This Freudian myth is not fanciful. Neither is it revolutionary in the history of ideas. It hews close to what common sense has led most people to expect in life: on the one hand, sexual instinct developing through involuntary maturation; on the other, civilization, society, moral controls, and even spiritual restraints. The dualism runs through all western philosophy; and the Judaeo-Christian tradition could hardly have existed without it. It is therefore a conventional, established, and even moderate way for human beings to think about their sexuality. It is, nevertheless, an unacceptable dualism. It is misleading in its interpretation of sexual behavior; and it is dangerous, even pernicious, in the morality it helps to found. For in identifying the sexual with the reproductive, it lends support to what Freud himself called "the tyranny of the genital." Freud continually recommended tolerance towards non-genital interests, but his doctrine arrogates to the genital a preferential status in all human sexuality. This would be justifiable if there were something in the nature of reproductive behavior which clearly *defined* sexual response as such. But the empirical data indicate nothing of the sort. Reproduction is only *one* of the goals of human sexuality, and only occasionally is it the principal one.

In defining the libido apart from society or civilization, Freud is motivated by a desire to link human sexuality to the sexuality of lower organisms from which we have evolved. In most of the mammalian species sexual behavior is automatic rather than deliberative, innate rather than learned, genetically programmed rather than socially determined. Rats who have been reared in complete isolation copulate in ways that are indistinguishable from the behavior of rats who have been reared in natural society.[4] But among primates the situation seems to be much more complex.[5] Chimpanzees who have not observed the mating behavior of other chimpanzees will not perform sexually until they have spent a long period in the company of prospective mates.[6] Harlow's experiments with rhesus monkeys suggest that playing with peers during childhood may also be a necessary condition for eventual sexuality.[7] Far from being instinctive in any pure and simple way, coitus and sexual desire in general seem to be a function of social arrangements into which these primates had to be introduced.

Once we get to human beings, cultural influences take on such importance that it becomes virtually impossible to separate sexual instinct from sexual learning in any reliable way. Freud and the Freudians admit, indeed insist upon, this. But for them the unity of sex and society merely means that the "overt manifestations" of the sexual instinct are culturally determined. Beneath the empirical phenomena the libido flows on in its own domain, even though we see it only through its transformations in society. If, however, primates require interaction with the group in order to be capable of copulation, and if human beings show an even greater dependence upon learning and acculturation for the expression of their sexuality, why *should* we postulate an unobservable libido that exists apart from environmental influences? Is it not preferable to define human sexuality in a more intimate relationship with human society, to see them as inextricably intermeshed without postulating a hypothetical residue?

I propose this alternative as a more faithful representation of the fact that human sexuality is pervasively conditioned by social and interpersonal needs as well as physiological processes. A savage who somehow survived in a wilderness without the company of other people would acquire the organic prerequisites for sexuality. In the case of a male, his genitals would grow, periodically fill with semen, and even discharge themselves through involuntary or masturbatory orgasm. But such experience would not be paradigmatic of human sexuality. For that is characteristically a way of using one's body to communicate—directly or indirectly—with some other person. Human sexuality generally occurs as a physical need for interpersonal contact. Even in autoeroticism, it is as if one has become a second person to oneself. Sexual behavior depends upon the organs of the body at each moment, and therefore the state of maturation is always crucial; but it is only as a sociobiological disposition that sexuality can be understood at any level of its being.

To reject the dualism between libido and society is also to recast the problem of repression. According to Freud, as well as thinkers like Marcuse and N. O. Brown, repression results from the reality principle throttling the human drive for sexual pleasure. It is society, particularly western civilization, damming up the libido and preventing it from achieving satisfactions related to organic development in the individual. If, however, one cannot separate libido and society, this model for explaining the phenomenon of repression is untenable. As long as one doubts that there is a unitary libido preordained by nature, one cannot assert that sexuality need only liberate itself of social interference in order to achieve its relevant consummations. There is also reason to think that repression depends upon restraints within sexuality itself as well as those from the outside; and if these inner restraints cannot be eliminated without damaging sexual response, we may have to reconsider the desirability of eliminating repression.

At the very least, our ideas about repression will have to be reformulated. Freud seemed to recognize this necessity in one or two places. In *Civilization and Its Discontents* he ends a chapter with these tantalizing words: "Sometimes one seems to perceive that it is not only the pressure of civilization but something in the nature of the [sexual] function itself which denies us full satisfaction and urges us along other paths. This may be wrong; it is hard to decide." [8] In a long footnote he then speculates about the possibility of there being an "organic repression" which developed in man along with the growth of civilization. This organic or inner repression he interprets as a defense against animal sexuality. Freud thinks it evolved in man when he assumed the erect gait and began to depreciate the sense of smell.

In the second of his three "Contributions to the Psychology of Love," Freud suggests another reason why the inner being of sexuality precludes absolute gratification. He remarks that "at its beginning sexual instinct is divided into a large number of components—or, rather, it develops from them—not all of which can be carried on into its final form; some have to be suppressed or turned to other uses before the final form results." [9] As an example of these suppressed components, Freud cites sadistic elements that belong to the instinct but have to be "abandoned." But if the libido develops by suppressing these components, one might have concluded that organic repression makes it *possible* for the final form of sexuality to achieve complete satisfaction. Although elements like the sadistic may be denied gratification in some respect, the sexual experience that results from such repression may be totally satisfying in view of what the organism demands at that moment. And if there is no one "final form"—as I am suggesting —neither can we say which are the components that must or should or will be abandoned in every case. The problem of repression thus becomes even more difficult than Freud imagined; and possibly that is why he terminates the discussion by ritualistically repeating his cardinal belief in the libido as a single, basic, unitary force: "All such developmental processes, however, relate only to the upper layers of the complicated structure. The fundamental processes which promote erotic impulse remain always the same." [10]

In questioning the essentialism of Freud, one need not eliminate words like "libidinal" from the English language. The adjectival form is useful as a synonym for "sexual," provided one realizes that it does not refer to a single something which is *the* libido or *the* sexual instinct. And once we discard the essentialistic concept, we may find that sexuality often involves inner restraints while civilization can be liberating as well as repressive. In the need for privacy, and in general the need to inhibit sexual response in various ways, one may discover the concrete instances of what Freud called organic repression. But, as I shall argue later in this book, these needs may also be related to social as well as biological factors that further human sexuality instead of merely restraining it.

Freud's ideas about organic repression have not had much influence on contemporary sexology. But the faith in a unitary substratum continues in Kinsey and Masters and Johnson whether or not they inherited it directly from Freud. These behavioral scientists are scarcely concerned with the libido per se. Kinsey does not list it in his index; and in their glossary, Masters and Johnson define it merely as "sexual drive or urge." [11] Nevertheless, these researchers insist upon an underlying uniformity of physiological response not only in male and female human beings, but also in all other mammals. Thus Kinsey begins by saying that the variations in individual sexual response "offer endless possibilities for combination and recombination," but then he immediately qualifies this by assertions about "basic" patterns: "Consequently the responses of each individual may be quite unlike those of any other individual, although the basic physiologic patterns of sexual response and orgasm are remarkably uniform among all individuals, both female and male, and throughout all of the species of mammals." [12] At times, Kinsey does sound as if he believed that there are many different patterns, all equally basic, but in his summary and conclusions he flatly states that "orgasm is a phenomenon which appears to be essentially the same in the human female and male." [13] On the next page he admits that this is somewhat surprising since in all the other mammalian species orgasm occurs only infrequently among the females. He does not seem to realize that this generalization contradicts what he has just been saying about the remarkable uniformity among all individuals in all of the species of mammals.

In Masters and Johnson, the belief in a physiologic oneness underlying the differences in sexual behavior recurs throughout their theory as well as their therapy. They think of the male as following a standard pattern of ejaculatory reaction, and they do not recognize any fundamental diversity within the characteristics of the female orgasm apart from duration and intensity. Although they provide three models for the female sexual response cycle, one of these is considered nonorgasmic and another is simply a reiteration of a sort that would occur in multiple orgasm. In its main configurations the orgasm is taken to be the same for all women, as it is for all men. Masters and Johnson are sometimes confusing about this since they often admit the existence of diversity even when they are arguing for uniformity. Speaking of quantitative and qualitative factors in the female orgasm, they say that these factors appear "totally variable between one woman's orgasmic experiences, and orgasm as it occurs in other women." But in the very next sentence they assert that "baseline physiologic reactions . . . remain consistent from orgasm to orgasm . . ." [14] They repeatedly insist that "basic orgasmic physiology" stays the same throughout all variations either in the modes of stimulation or in the individual responses that different women undergo. Obviously, the words "baseline" and "basic" are crucial here. Whatever else they mean, these terms bespeak a uniformity despite the apparent evidences of diversity.

What is the justification for believing in this fundamental uniformity? In discussing their method of approach, Masters and Johnson begin by listing two questions that guided their research: "What physical reactions develop as the human male and female respond to effective sexual stimulation? Why do men and women behave as they do when responding to effective sexual stimulation?" [15] Throughout their writing, the phrase "effective sexual stimulation" occurs time and time again. In fact, it contains within it the core of Masters' and Johnson's essentialism. For their investigation is always directed towards selected patterns of response, and only behavior that leads to these patterns is considered effective sexual stimulation. No other behavior, however characteristic or satisfying it may be, is taken to be definitive of "the sexual cycle." To say then that the physiology of male or female orgasm is basically the same is merely to articulate the consequences of limiting oneself to a single model for each. Everything else having been eliminated from a previously determined category of *effective* stimulation, diversity in the basic physiology has been ruled out in advance. And since this preferred system of biologic response defines the very nature of human sexuality as Masters and Johnson see it, we are back to a nonverifiable faith not too dissimilar from Freud's belief in an underlying libido.

The consequences of holding this faith appear at various places in Masters' and Johnson's investigation. It affects the choice of study-subjects whom they admit to their research population, and it affects the generalizations which they derive from their observations. They themselves list several criteria for admission which created "selectivity" in the research population. The most important of these criteria is what they call "facility of sexual responsiveness." [16] In other words, the subjects under observation would have to be those whose sexual performance matched the prior conditions incorporated in the concept of effective stimulation. And though Masters and Johnson were working with a "small, arbitrarily selected segment of male and female society" (as they freely confess), their general conclusions would seem to have been guided by what they assumed that human sexuality *must* be like: "Attempts to answer the challenge inherent in the question, 'What do men and women do in response to effective sexual stimulation?' have emphasized the *similarities, not the differences,* in the anatomy and physiology of human sexual response." [17] [Their italics.] In saying this, Masters and Johnson are extrapolating from their particular sample, in which the similarities may very well have been more noteworthy than the differences. But if one is to talk about human sexuality as a whole, one must also emphasize basic differences that Masters and Johnson neglect or minimize because they did not observe them.

If one sought to describe and analyze the empirical data with a maximum fidelity, there would be no need for either Freud's essentialism or Masters' and Johnson's. One would merely delineate the diverse and often irreducible patterns of response which presented themselves to careful observation. One might also make recommendations, but they would not be the same for all people on all occasions. The pluralistic attitude which I am advocating employs that approach as a corrective to the biases and falsifications that essentialism frequently creates. The pluralistic approach is needed as a way of resolving all problems about human sexuality, but possibly the question of the orgasm more than most. For if we understand the nature of the orgasm, we learn a great deal about the elusive goals of sexual response. And though men and women also cherish other elements in their erotic experience, the orgasm serves as an obvious evidence of sexual culmination. It is a consummation which reveals much of what we mean by human sexuality.

We must ask ourselves, however, whether the orgasm is a single entity or a diversity of responses referred to by a single word, whether it is similar for male and female, whether it is the most important consummation, and whether it is or is not the goal for all sexual experience that people have considered successful and wholly satisfying. We must also ask ourselves what is the relationship between the orgasm and concepts of "sexual relief" or "release of sexual tension." Built into all these concepts is the idea of an organic distress which may lead to behavioral responses that eventuate in a satisfying and life-enhancing resolution. Kinsey speaks of "a quiescence, a calm, a peace, a satisfaction with the world which, in the minds of many persons, is the most notable aspect of any type of sexual activity." [18] He uses these words to describe the postorgasmic state, but we may wonder whether they are true of all orgasms, and whether they are true of no responses other than the orgasm. On the basis of his clinical work with thousands of patients, Jan Raboch reports that "only roughly a quarter of the women in whom the capacity for orgasms is greatly reduced or absent, remained unsatisfied after coitus, or were inwardly disturbed or tense; three-quarters of them did not subjectively miss orgasms." [19]

Given this kind of evidence, one would like to know what is meant—not only by Raboch's patients, but also by people in general—when reference is made to satisfaction and its occurrence with or without an orgasm. To define the orgasm as "the peak of sexual excitement during sexual activity" (a definition that occurs in the glossary of the book from which I quoted Raboch) is of no use since we do not know what kind of peak truly matters.[20] Furthermore, concepts of consummation or sexual release involve physiological as well as psychological coordinates. Ordinarily we assume that satisfaction will be something physical as well as something that is felt. But the relationship between the physiological and the psychological is a problem of major importance to the scientist as well as the philosopher. And in relation to the orgasm, one often encounters situations in which psychological and physiological criteria seem to conflict. Some women show a physiological reaction characteristic of the orgasm but claim to be sexually unsatisfied; others report complete satisfaction although their behavioral responses would have led many physiologists to deny that they could be having an orgasm. If we admit all the variations, we run a risk of allowing too much into our conception of sexual release. But if we exclude or minimize the differences between individual consummations, we return to the essentialism we are trying to escape.

Through the careful use of sexual pluralism, we may be able to avoid both extremes. I see no other way to advance beyond the morass in which sexological theory finds itself at present.

Chapter 1

TOWARDS
SEXUAL PLURALISM

In an article written almost twenty years ago, Albert Ellis questioned the Freudian claim that there are two distinct kinds of sexual orgasms in women. Asking whether the vaginal orgasm may not actually be a myth, he presented evidence for and against believing that it exists. He then said: "There is certainly no evidence that women who may only or mainly have an orgasm through clitoral manipulation are emotionally immature or disturbed; and there is considerable suggestive evidence that they are no more disturbed than are women who may only have an orgasm through intravaginal stimulation." [1]

At the time he was writing, Ellis had reason to attack the Freudian position. For in effect it imposed a tyranny upon all women who accepted the medical authority of psychiatry in general. Those women who had never experienced what they themselves would call a "vaginal orgasm" often considered themselves inferior; and those who experienced orgasm only or mainly through clitoral manipulation were encouraged to believe that whatever difficulties in life they might have were either directly or indirectly related to their sexual phenomenology. In fact, as Ellis says, the psychiatric dogma not only convinced many women who did not have orgasms through intravaginal stimulation that they were imperfect or immature as women, but also it was the kind of belief that could "easily *make* such women emotionally and sexually disturbed." [2] [His italics.]

In the years that have intervened, the tyranny of the vaginal orgasm has been combatted very effectively by various segments of the sexological community. Theorists other than Ellis have often taken up the attack, asserting that "an orgasm is an orgasm" and that all orgasms release sexual tension equally well; popular and polemical writers, like the radical wing of the women's liberation movement, have insisted that women who claim to have vaginal orgasms are deluding themselves in the service of a male ideology; and experimental sexologists, like Masters and Johnson, have denied that there is any biological basis for distinguishing between two kinds of orgasms of the sort that the Freudians had in mind. This position, which has now become as authoritative and orthodox as the one it was opposing, reduces all orgasmic experience to a function of clitoral sensitivity. In short, the earlier dogma has been countered by one that is opposite and no less extreme, an antithesis that may be just as tyrannical as the thesis it sought to undermine. One may now ask, changing the crucial word in Ellis' original question: Is the *clitoral* orgasm a myth?

This question is not asked with any intention of denying that women have orgasms resulting merely from the stimulation of the clitoris, or even that the clitoris has the great importance in sexual behavior that the received opinion nowadays assigns to it. Rather it is posed for the sake of questioning the idea that *all* orgasmic response is a function primarily of stimulation and physiological reaction in the clitoris. Anne Koedt, just to mention one of many who affirm the current orthodoxy, insists that "there is only one area for sexual climax although there are many areas for sexual arousal; that area is the clitoris. All orgasms are extensions of sensations from this area." [3] On this view, women have two separate biological functions: one is reproductive, and that involves the vagina, but in itself the vagina is not sensitive as a sexual organ; the other is distinctively sexual, and that depends upon the clitoris as an organ whose response to stimulation explains the very possibility of female orgasm.

This new orthodoxy is as tyrannical as the one that preceded it because it too assumes that all women must be the same in their sexuality. Where the Freudians emphasized the differences between male and female, and therefore concluded that women who resembled men in their sexual inclinations were somehow sick or abnormal, the counterposition emphasizes the similarities between male and female—the clitoris being homologous to the penis—with the result that women whose responsiveness is quite different from a man's can only conclude that they are inferior or incomplete in some respect. The only way to avoid either the old or the new form of tyranny is to recognize that women are *not* all alike, that in some ways the sexual responsiveness of women does resemble the male's, but that this is not equally true of all women, and that for many women sexuality entails satisfying and health-giving responses which involve a physiological pattern quite different from the kind of sexuality which centers upon the clitoris.

We may also point out that the male is not a unitary sexological entity either. There is no single nature or unique condition that defines his sexuality. His responses often resemble the female's in some respects, but not wholly or invariably. And while we may eventually delineate patterns of male psychology and physiology, there is among them no one pattern or response—unless it be ejaculation itself—which is more definitive of the male orgasm than any other. As there is no essential female, neither is there an essential male.

In studying problems related to the nature of the female orgasm, physiologists have often assumed that there must be a single biological pattern common to all women who experience orgasm, as there must be a basic biological uniformity for digestion, defecation, parturition, and so on. They also assumed that within certain limits there will be a correlation between the physiological stimuli and the reports that women normally give in describing their experiences. Thus if a woman is stimulated in a manner that brings about the physiological pattern definitive of the orgasm, she can be expected to have specific feelings that she will generally recognize as the feelings that belong to the having of an orgasm. These assumptions are not unreasonable, and a great deal of medical practice relies upon assumptions of a similar sort. In the case of the female orgasm, however, they are simply inappropriate. For in giving their reports, women have described their feelings in highly divergent ways; and even in the details of reproductive physiology, there is not—as we shall see—a single system that covers everything that women have recognized as being orgasmic.

The sexologist must therefore choose between three alternatives. First, he may define orgasm in psychological terms that are so broad that they can encompass not only a wide range of sexual experiences but also a considerable diversity of physiological processes. It was this approach that characterized sexology prior to Kinsey and Masters and Johnson. Even as late as 1968, one finds scientists like Udry and Morris defining female orgasm as "a high peak of sexual excitement followed by sudden relaxation." [4] This is general enough to cover almost everything that anyone would want to call an orgasm, but it is so vague and panoramic that it tells us very little about the condition it purports to define.

The second approach is represented by the attempt of Masters and Johnson to impose some rigor and clarity upon the characterization of female orgasm. They deal with the orgasm as part of a regular sequence in female sexual response, a stage that follows upon the excitement and plateau phases and precedes the resolution phase. The orgasm itself they describe as vasocongestion issuing into rhythmic release through recurrent muscular contractions in the outer third of the vagina. Masters and Johnson do not provide a short definition, but Sherfey represents them accurately when she says: "The nature of the orgasm is the same regardless of the erotogenic zone stimulated to produce it. The orgasm consists of the rhythmic contractions of the extravaginal musculature against the greatly distended circumvaginal venous plexi and vestibular bulbs surrounding the lower third of the vagina." [5] For Masters and Johnson these rhythmic contractions serve as criteria for the occurrence of orgasm. Though most of their work is physiological, they also claim to have discovered experiential correlations. They associate the orgasmic release of vasocongestion with sensations of "suspension or stoppage," "suffusion of warmth," and the actual feeling of involuntary contractions or "pelvic throbbing." [6]

This second approach, superior as it is to anything in the literature that preceded it, fails to account for the fact that many women report having orgasms although they do not experience the rhythmic contractions. Pomeroy has recently suggested that such contractions may occur without either the woman or her partner being aware of them.[7] And possibly this is true for minimal or borderline cases of what Masters and Johnson consider to be orgasms. But in the clear cases, there is no reason to think that so powerful a physiological response could occur without the woman's feeling it. Consequently one must be at least puzzled by the insistence of women who claim to have strong and unmistakable experiences of orgasm without any awareness of the contractions Masters and Johnson describe. Not many investigators have considered this problem, but Edward Elkan, who has, states quite emphatically that "contractions of the vaginal muscles and of those forming the pelvic floor are frequently reported, but in an equal number of other cases nothing is known about muscular contractions even in the course of the strongest orgasm." [8]

What are we to say of such women? If they *claim* to have had an orgasm, who is to deny that they have actually had one? Of course, it is possible that their experience is too impoverished for them to realize what a complete sexual release would be like. One can imagine young girls who *think* they have orgasms simply because they find coitus rather enjoyable even though they have never had the kind of peak and subsequent relaxation which will eventually come to them with greater maturity. But many of the women who say that they have orgasms without contractions are quite mature and sexually sophisticated, and some of them have also experienced orgasms that were accompanied by the relevant contractions. If such a woman reports having orgasms that do not involve the physiological processes which Masters and Johnson take to be definitive, it seems plausible to think that Masters and Johnson have limited themselves to a definition that falsifies the actual diversity of physiological and psychological events which make up the female orgasm. In other words, they have attained their admirable degree of rigor at the expense of eliminating everything that does not fit into a fairly arbitrary category.

The third approach, which is the one that I am advocating, starts with the idea that terms like "consummation" and "orgasm" require a pluralistic analysis. One may say that such words refer to a release of sexual tension and that in this respect there is no difference between male and female orgasm; but having said this, we must then point out that men and women differ in the ways in which they attain sexual release. For a man, the experience is generally directed towards ejaculation. For a woman, something similar often occurs inasmuch as the contractions characteristic of *some* orgasms resemble the muscular contractions which propel the semen forth. But women have a reproductive function that sets them apart from the male, and their sexual satisfaction will often depend upon responses that are quite different from anything a man could have.

It is not enough, however, to argue for the pluralistic character of orgasms in general. For within any type of orgasm, whether it be male or female, there will be as many variations as there are emotional responses to another human being at the moments of physical and psychological intimacy. One might almost say that this is true of all human consummations. How many ways are there to see a sunset or to enjoy a great work of art? Such responses may be analyzed into categories, but our analysis must never forget that consummatory events are always unique—never the same and often very different.

As a first step towards sexual pluralism, consider questions about the locus of stimulation necessary for the achievement of female orgasm. Some of those who believe that all orgasms are really clitoral orgasms mean by this that the proper stimulation of the clitoris is all that is required for a woman to have an orgasm. And that is true inasmuch as muscular contractions and a corresponding sense of release can be induced through clitoral caresses whether or not they are accompanied by coitus. The caressing is all that most women need in order to have *an* orgasm. But in coitus, the clitoris is not directly stimulated and even if it is inadvertently massaged by the thrusting of the penis and the tugging of the labia, it is not always the principal locus of stimulation. In some orgasms the cervix and possibly the peritoneum are more important, and more obviously the loci of direct stimulation. It is for this reason that many women who are incapable of experiencing orgasm through the manual stimulation of the clitoris, women who feel sexual excitement when their clitoris is stimulated but no release of tension, are nevertheless able to experience orgasmic sensations as a result of coital experience. These sensations may have little or no localization in the clitoris, and they are often reported as being felt deep within the abdomen. In subsequent chapters, we shall return to this kind of evidence in various contexts.

As a response to such evidence, those who believe that there is only one kind of orgasm and that it must be characterized by contractions in the outer third of the vagina seek to distinguish between the objective nature of sexual events and the subjective or psychic evaluation which a woman may put upon them. On this view, what is happening to all women who have orgasms is more or less the same, but satisfaction will vary in accordance with one or another cathexis of emotion. If the woman's upbringing or social acculturation leads her to prefer coitus—for whatever reason —she will consider coital orgasms as superior to, and consequently different from, the ones attained by means of clitoral masturbation. Kinsey cites the "psychologic satisfaction in knowing that a sexual union and deep penetration have been effected" as a reason why some women prefer coital experience.[9] He then goes on to say that "the realization that the partner is being satisfied may be a factor of considerable importance here." More recent writers, particularly among the radical women liberationists, claim that coitus has been foisted upon women by men who care only for the fact that the vagina provides an optimal massage for the penis, even though the woman may experience little that is sexually satisfying to her. Presumably she submits to the relationship as a way of conforming to the demands of male-dominated society.

This line of reasoning seems wildly speculative and wholly far-fetched, although it may have some plausibility if one thinks of female sexual behavior *apart* from the phenomenon of orgasm. Given the fact that many societies have brought up their women to think of themselves as reproductive machinery that had no rights to sexual pleasure of the sort that men enjoyed, it doubtless is the case that many women submitted to sexual intercourse merely as a means of accommodating the husband. But even in the most repressive of societies, there must have been women who acquired habits of responsiveness that would enable them to achieve orgasmic satisfaction while they were also satisfying their husbands. Conditioned by social and psychological circumstances as they may have been, these sexual responses would still involve a diversity of physiological patterns. Instead of thinking that orgasms are all alike but women evaluate them differently, it seems more reasonable to assume that evaluations differ because different women, or the same woman on different occasions, have different predilections among the physiological responses which are available to them.

It is also possible that Masters and Johnson—to say nothing of their less authoritative followers—are themselves imposing subjective evaluations upon the physiological events they observe. And this can have important consequences in therapy, and in society as a whole. One encourages sexual conformity if one tells women that their experiences are not *truly* orgasmic unless they fit some particular pattern. An assertion of this kind, like the Victorian view that women ought not to have orgasms at all, fosters a reorientation of attitude and thereby tends to change sexual behavior in a single direction. It may not prevent women from having orgasms which are physically as well as psychologically diverse, but it can cause a woman who might otherwise have interpreted her consummatory experience as a proof of femininity to wonder whether she is even "normal."

In trying to avoid both the Freudian and the anti-Freudian forms of tyranny, it is important to recognize that each purports to be scientific although both are motivated by that kind of prescriptivism which Kate Millett calls "sexual politics." [10] Miss Millett rightly insists upon the normative character of Freud's analysis, but she fails to see that those sexologists whose opinions she prefers are no less normative in what they say about female sexuality. Thus Freud is indeed leading the argument towards presuppositions about what *he* considers normal in women when he calls masturbation an essentially masculine activity, when he suggests that the transfer of interest from the clitoris to the vagina belongs to the essence of femininity, when he associates this necessary transfer with an acceptance of passivity and supine submissiveness on the part of the woman, and when he derives from all of this the social conclusions with which he clearly began— conclusions that assign the intellectual and managerial roles in life to men while relegating the functions of child-rearing and domesticity to women. But surely Masters and Johnson are foot soldiers in an ideological cause no less than Freud, even though they may not always recognize the tendentious character of their generalizations. In claiming that all coital orgasms are physiologically indistinguishable from noncoital ones, they take as their norm a preferred sample of the female population—i.e., women who have been selected on the basis of their ability to induce the prescribed contractions under observation and with facility in both masturbation and coitus. Masters and Johnson ignore evidence, which in fact their methodology discounts *a priori*, about women who do not have this facility but nevertheless find that coitus provides a sexual release quite different from the pleasures of masturbation. Moreover, there is reason to believe that women who do have the required facility are probably unrepresentative of women as a whole. As indicated by figures which Gebhard has recently provided, the mere occurrence of masturbation is by no means universal among women:

> According to our data 28 percent of fifteen-year-old girls have experience of masturbation (with or without orgasm), up to the age of twenty roughly 40 percent, and up to forty 62 percent of all women have masturbated at some time in their lives.[11]

By treating their sample as the norm, Masters and Johnson are— in effect—*redefining* the concept of what is biologically relevant to sexual satisfaction. Only a particular kind of woman is taken as the exemplar of female sexuality, and it is not too surprising that as a human being she differs considerably from the kind of woman the Freudians idealized.

In Mary Jane Sherfey, one of the theorists who try to apply the research of Masters and Johnson to broader sexological speculation, the normative bias is even more obvious. Starting with the fact that women sometimes have multiple orgasms but without a sense of total satisfaction, Sherfey concludes that women in general cannot be wholly satiated regardless of how many orgasms they have, and in fact that by their nature they are *inherently* and *essentially* insatiable:

> No doubt the most far-reaching hypothesis extrapolated from these biological data is the existence of the universal and physically normal condition of women's inability ever to reach complete sexual satiation in the presence of the most intense, repetitive orgasmic experiences, no matter how produced. Theoretically, a woman could go on having orgasms indefinitely if physical exhaustion did not intervene.[12]

A statement of this sort, presented this way, looks as if it is merely an empirical generalization, a scientific hypothesis that might be true or false depending on the evidence. But that this is not so becomes apparent when Sherfey admits, indeed "stresses," that by the term "sexual satiation" she does not mean *satisfaction*. A woman may be "satisfied to the full," she says, in a great many situations, some of which need not even be orgasmic. But according to Sherfey, satisfaction is an unreliable guide to satiation, because far from indicating the culmination of a biological process, the former merely reveals the woman's decision to *consider* herself satisfied. Speaking of the difference between male and female orgasm, Sherfey says:

> The man *is* satisfied. The woman *usually wills* herself to be satisfied because she is simply unaware of the extent of her orgasmic capacity . . . this hypothesis will come as no great shock to many women who consciously realize, or intuitively sense, their lack of satiation.[13] [Her italics.]

No, it will not. But it will come as a shock to many other women who consciously realize and intuitively sense that their orgasms are wholly satisfying, even if they are said to be lacking in something else called satiation. Sherfey assures us that in all women there must be a lack of satiation, but her distinction between satisfaction and satiation seems purely fanciful. To say that women *cannot* have an orgasm which alleviates their sexual tension as completely and thoroughly as the orgasm does for the male is simply to ignore the vast number of reports from women who claim to have such orgasms quite regularly.[14] Sherfey's generalization would seem to be based upon the condition of women whom the Freudians often denigrated by calling them "clitoridal" or even "nymphomaniacal." A so-called nymphomaniac may have orgasms, but they do not satisfy sufficiently to terminate her sexual craving. The Freudians did no service to such women by simply considering their kind of sexuality abnormal or pathological. There may even be something in the nature of some orgasms (which we shall be discussing) that gives credence to Sherfey's belief that women who have those orgasms will not be satisfied in any terminative way. But from this fact, together with the evidence about women who have other kinds of orgasms, we can only conclude that no one female disposition is uniquely indicative of what it is to be a woman, of what she is essentially or by her biological nature. How could one justifiably convince a woman that she has merely *willed* herself into a state of total satisfaction? It seems more likely that a woman who says she is fully satisfied has had a different type of sexual experience from one who terminates her series of multiple orgasms out of physical fatigue even though she might prefer to continue. We have no need, and in fact no right, to make either experience definitive of what *all* women are like.

Sherfey is seduced into her peculiar brand of mythological thinking by the assumption that there must be for women something called a "biological orgasmic capacity." Finding that some women can have fifty, a hundred, even two hundred orgasms one after the other, and that these women stop when they do out of mere physical exhaustion, she claims to have discovered something that belongs to the essence of the female orgasm itself—namely, that by its very nature it is nonterminative. But facts about particular women on particular occasions need not apply to all women on all occasions. A biological capacity that some women sometimes have is not the same as a biological capacity in the female sex as a whole.

The extremes of both Freudian and anti-Freudian sexology are responsible for more than just the feelings of inadequacy which they create in one or another kind of woman. They also authorize inauthentic responses that people undergo in order to express their sexuality in the "approved" manner—whatever that manner may be. Psychiatrists like Marie Robinson and Anthony Storr encourage men to be aggressive in their coital technique at the same time as they demand a corresponding submissiveness on the part of the female.[15] On the other hand, the techniques that Masters and Johnson recommend discourage the male's aggressiveness while accentuating the female's.[16] Their concept of "give-to-get" implies an equality of aggressive pleasuring designed to afford the female a sexual freedom equivalent to what the Freudians generally limited to the male. Each partner is to take turns in giving pleasure and in getting it from the other. The woman is no longer to submit to the male's leadership in order to get the sensuous enjoyment that she desires, nor is she to restrain herself from giving him whatever pleasures he may want. If the Freudian ideology insisted that men and women were bound in their legitimate responses by predetermined instincts, their critics insist upon total liberation from all sexual restraints and from all assumptions about instinctual differences between the sexes.

As often happens in the history of ideas, neither the thesis nor the antithesis is necessarily mistaken. These two opposing sexological theories are both right inasmuch as they call attention to important facets of human nature. They are both wrong, however, inasmuch as they generalize a partial truth as if it were applicable to all men and women. Thus it is undoubtedly the case that men receive hormonal inducement to sexual aggressiveness of a sort that women do not. But the Freudians are not justified in concluding from this fact that men will be psychologically disturbed or even repressed if they employ coital techniques which minimize their aggressiveness. The psychiatrist Natalie Shainess has criticized Masters and Johnson on the grounds that devices such as their "squeeze technique" for ejaculatory control are joyless and ignore the psychological forces at work.[17] And certainly the squeeze technique, just to limit ourselves to this concrete illustration, does prevent the male from venting his aggressive inclinations with any degree of spontaneity. But in itself neither this nor any other technique is necessarily harmful. One would like to know whether the man is troubled by his aggressiveness towards the female, and whether he would mind being less spontaneous. On the other hand, it could be most unfortunate if a couple used the squeeze technique on the assumption that the man must be sexually inadequate simply because he ejaculates within a specified number of minutes, or before the woman has had her own orgasm. It would also be unfortunate if it were recommended for a man who either liked being aggressive in relation to a woman who also liked his aggressiveness, or—what is more relevant nowadays—for a man who would benefit from being encouraged to accept his native aggressiveness to a greater extent than he may already. Not only must one consider both partners in the sexual relationship, but also one must realize that human beings are too complex for anyone to know in advance what will constitute libidinal success or even the type of consummation that might or might not be attainable.

Once we accept the pluralistic point of view, it becomes unnecessary to see the sexual situation as either reactionary males or radical females do. If it is not in the nature of a man to respond in any one way to his aggressive need for dominance, neither does he have to view a woman who wishes to dominate as a necessary threat to his virility. Such women were called "viriloid" or "masculine" by Freudians like Marie Bonaparte and Helene Deutsch on the assumption that only males were justified in being aggressive or seeking dominance.[18] The justification derived from the male's nature, his sheer biological configuration. But if there is no biological nature which predetermines any single response as necessarily preferable to all others, we need not assume that women who wish to behave aggressively are thereby distorting their femininity or destroying their inherent capacity as sexual beings. There is no reason to believe, as Deutsch maintains, that women can have satisfying orgasms only if they school themselves in what she calls "the proper management of feminine masochism." [19] On the other hand, liberationists are out of touch with the great mass of women when they condemn "the institution of sexual intercourse" as being something that men have created for their own purposes alone.[20] In saying this, these writers mean that men have *forced* women, deluded them, into thinking that vaginal stimulation is the epitome of female satisfaction. And since there is no such thing as *the* epitome in human sexuality, but only at best one or another kind of enjoyment available at one or another moment, this complaint is worth making. It is a tragic mistake, however, to think that the more a woman has liberated herself from male dominance the more she will disdain coital experience. Women who make this assertion are merely duplicating that indifference to female well-being for which they tax the male. No theory, and possibly no political cause, has a right to discourage any woman from experiencing pleasures that have meant so much to so many women.

In the following chapters, I shall explore the possibilities of pluralism in relation to various problems about male and female sexuality. We begin with a distinction between two attitudes or modes of sexuality that belong to the responsiveness of all human beings and that contribute to the great diversity of erotic consummations. I call them "the sensuous" and "the passionate."

Chapter 2

———◆·◆———

THE SENSUOUS AND
THE PASSIONATE

There are many ways in which human sexuality can be analyzed. In distinguishing between the sensuous and the passionate, I refer to elements that occur in everyone's experience but often at different times and in different ways. We encounter one another through our senses, and we enjoy the encounter only as they are gratified. We perceive each other through our ability to see, to touch, to hear, to smell, and even to taste. Our sensations are generally localized in specific areas of the body, even though they contribute to responses that unify them into a single system of pleasurability. In sexual behavior, a man or woman may concentrate upon sensory pleasure and even seek to prolong it indefinitely; they may give it special importance in their life together, bestow value upon it, create ideals that dignify and further its occurrence. For some people, sexual experience amounts to little more than the sensuous, and even the end-pleasure of orgasmic relief becomes subordinate to the delights of sensory enjoyment. For others, however, sexuality is charged (on some occasions at least) with emotions of yearning, craving, hope, anticipation, joy, oneness: overwhelming tension followed by a dying or dissipation of feeling, a final release of sexual energies.

This variable complex of warm and turbulent emotions—in contrast to the cooler and less demanding ones that characterize the sensuous—has always been recognized as the passionate aspect of sexuality. But its relationship to instinct or innate patterns of response has never been understood, nor its dependence upon cultural and environmental influence, nor even its relationship to the sensuous element. For the passionate requires at least a modicum of the sensuous in order for it to occur. Erotic emotions are always mediated by some form of sensory experience, which then becomes submerged in the needs and consummations of the passionate mode. For its part, the sensuous would not be felt as something sexual that relates us to another human being unless it also involved the passionate to some degree. The two elements may be contrasted, but one need not assume that they exist in perfect isolation even though they define different attitudes. And while these sexual attitudes may approximate a virtual independence, they may also cooperate harmoniously within a person's experience.

When the sensuous and the passionate become alienated from one another, those who believe in passion tend to think of the sensuous as evil or undesirable. In English the word "sensual" bears that connotation. For their part, those who believe in the sensuous often feel that the passionate is emotionally aberrant, romantic in a bad sense. But these negative judgments are unreliable. There is nothing necessarily good or bad about either aspect of sexuality. And nothing, even in their unfortunate isolation, prevents either one from being administered with love. For that term refers to the *manner* in which we relate to other people, *how* we are sensuous or passionate towards them. Perhaps the confusion about love results from the fact that "falling in love" implies a violence of emotional involvement that bespeaks the passionate and sometimes excludes the sensuous. But falling in love is not the only kind of love, and frequently it is not really love at all. When it entails no clear perception of the other person, it is not love; when it is determined by the lover's need but not the beloved's welfare, it is not love; when it is possessive rather than being a bestowal of value, it is not love. To love another person passionately, one must have both love and passion for that person. But the two are different, and passion alone is no guarantee of love.

On the other hand, we often use the word "love" to mean a sensuous interest that one person may have in another. This may or may not be a misuse of the other person; and it may or may not be love in the honorific sense that word usually implies. The sensuous is closely related to the playful. But one can play with someone either as a cat plays with a mouse or as a doting mother plays with her baby. Play can be destructive or creative, a murderous confrontation or a joyous interaction. When it effects a mutuality of enjoyment, the sensuous belongs to a loving attitude no less than the passionate—and whether or not it is accompanied by the passionate.

In the western world the sensuous and the passionate have often been pitted against one another. Each has been idealized by some people and denigrated by others. For the last two thousand years their partisans have fought in constant warfare against each other. All men and women have participated in the battle; and all have suffered for it. One cannot hope to find a single reason for the struggle. At different times, different attitudes have prevailed; and later developments served as reactions to earlier ones. Before describing the psychodynamics of the conflict, I shall trace the history of its development—but without trying to find one or only one means of explaining it.

If it seems strange to say that love can be sexual and yet not passionate, the reason can be found in ideas we have inherited from the past. We have been taught to believe that love as something desirable takes us beyond the pleasures of the senses. The very concept of love as a condition worthy of aspiration arose among people who were ashamed of their bodies. They therefore sought to dignify sex by interpreting it as an ardent desire for something else. In the *Phaedrus*, for example, Plato begins with a paradigmatic situation of sexual interest between two persons. The sensuous components he discounts as merely physical, but the passionate obviously intrigues him. That the lover *yearns* for the beloved signifies to him a search for goodness which underlies all empirical nature. Once the lovers purify their passion by directing it towards the good itself, their relationship becomes what Plato calls "true love." Without this transcendental function, passion could only be self-indulgent lust, a burning appetite that can never be satisfied. As such, it was something to be feared, avoided, cured, and exorcised like all the other evils of the body. In the ancient world, passion was often related to insanity. But also it symbolized a "divine madness" that took men out of themselves and enabled them to communicate with the gods. Plato eliminates the materiality of passion by directing it towards an ideal entity—the Good or Beautiful. This preserved the value of the passionate, but at the expense of making it inhuman and *non-sexual*. The Good is not a person, and we cannot desire it as we would desire another human being.

In its attempt to rectify the deficiencies of Greek philosophy, Christianity merged Platonism with the mystery religions of antiquity. These had celebrated the passional element of sex both in itself and as the means to oneness with a personal deity. Like Platonism, Christianity condemned sexual passion; but like the pagan mysteries, it cultivated the passionate striving for God. In effect, it tried to satisfy human passions by means of the mystical encounter. Though later theologians modified the original design, Christianity conceived of man's love for God as a passionate experience that would make all other passionate experiences unnecessary. Not only unnecessary but even harmful to the soul and actually sinful. With this restriction the ideal of passion survived though greatly transmuted, for now it belonged to love directed towards a spiritual entity. But since that entity was a person, a Supreme Being and yet a person all the same, the ideal could still involve passion not *wholly* different from the passion in sexuality. As Christ had given himself in the nonsexual agony of his Passion, so too would the devout believer achieve salvation through a love that duplicates the union of two passionate lovers but does so at the higher level of pure spirituality.

There were two unfortunate consequences that followed upon the Christian idealization of passion. First, it meant that passionate experience as something good was reserved for the love of God to the exclusion of everything and everyone else. Second, it meant that passion directed towards any other object would have to be utterly prohibited. For the ancient world, passion was frightening because it withdrew a man from society and the influence of other men. But for Christianity its occurrence in sexuality was even worse: a sacrilege towards God himself. It is in this context that one must understand Saint Jerome's dictum that "he who loves his own wife too ardently is an adulterer." Since the legitimate spouse is really God, passion directed towards another —even the woman one has married in church—is adultery *more* terrible than when a married man sleeps with someone who is not his wife. "A wise man ought to love his wife with judgment, not with passion. Let a man govern his voluptuous impulses, and not rush headlong into intercourse." [1]

This opinion of Saint Jerome was repeated by all the doctors of the Church in the Middle Ages. Sexuality as such was not the enemy they fought. They feared, and therefore considered diabolical, the very possibility of passionate love between human beings. When Saint Paul said it is better to marry than to burn, he spoke as one who wished to avoid the pleasures as well as the pains of burning. Marriage being a sacrament, the conjugal act could not be evil in itself. Indeed, it was a meritorious means of propagating the species. Nor did most thinkers believe that sexual impulse was sinful. Although there was much debate about whether desire for sexual intercourse preceded the Fall of Adam and whether it was original sin or merely the punishment for original sin, medieval philosophers and theologians generally agreed that sexuality— properly administered—could be innocent. Saint Thomas insisted that neither the desire for sexual pleasure nor even the pleasure itself was evil, but only the subordination of reason to emotionality which often accompanied them. It was the passionate element that deflected man from his rational search for the Highest Good, thereby leading him into sin or mortal error.

It followed from this position that the sensuous could still find a place in Christianity. Sex being a natural function of man, his sensuous pleasures merely indicated that he was doing what he was made to do with the enjoyment that comes from efficiency. The sensuous was not to be pursued for its own sake, but nothing prevented it from belonging to a life in which everything happened for the sake of God. As long as personal emotions did not intrude, bodily pleasure was morally of little interest to the Church; and in fact, the sensuous was never condemned in the way that passional sex was. As a result, the split between the modes of sexuality hardened even further; and when the humanization of Christian doctrine occurred in the late Middle Ages, it too divided into two separate camps. On the one hand, there were those who tried to elevate the love of man and woman by duplicating within its structure the same passionate devotion that the Church reserved for the love of God. The heresy of courtly love, in the troubadours for example, consisted in the desire to treat a woman with the same spiritual yearning that only God deserved. Though the troubadours generally considered themselves good Christians, the Church attacked their humanism as an insidious mockery of orthodox doctrine.

On the other hand, there were those who capitalized upon Christianity's acceptance of the sensuous to make it the principal focus of sexual experience. Alongside of courtly love there developed a lusty and carefree attitude towards the nonpassional pleasures of sex. Goliardic poetry is filled with it. In the *Carmina Burana* we see its infiltration into the monastery; in Boccaccio and Chaucer it dominates the *Decameron* and *The Canterbury Tales*, though not the *Filostrato* or *Troilus and Criseyde*, which belong to the passionate element. In the *Roman de la Rose*, the first part celebrates the passions of courtly love while the second part (written by another hand) reviles them for the greater glory of the sensuous. Within the writings of even the earliest troubadours— Guillaume IX, Marcabru, Cavalcanti, and many others—the two approaches to sexual love occur together, always separate and distinct but coexisting as viable alternatives in human relations. Though the troubadours generally favored the passionate over the sensuous, some of their poems make us wonder about their ultimate preference. And by the time we reach the Renaissance, it is often impossible—as in the love songs of Lorenzo de' Medici—to determine which of the two attitudes is authentic and which is merely a poetic façade. Sometimes the two are blended and thoroughly harmonized with one another, in Lorenzo's poetry as well as in the writings of other Renaissance authors.

For the most part, the modern world has retained the division that began in the Middle Ages. Luther and the Reformation as a whole reversed the earlier tradition in Christianity by considering the sensuous to be ultimately as sinful as the passionate. But also, Luther treated sexuality as a natural appetite that became dangerous only when its frustration gave it undue importance. It was to be satisfied (twice a week) with a regularity that made emotional extravagance impossible. At the same time, however, Luther unwittingly enabled the passionate to flourish in a way that it never had before. For in arguing that man could not hope to love God, Luther concluded that God's love descended to the level of humanity and showed itself in the ardent bonds that drew one person to another. This love could manifest itself in society at large but also between men and women, particularly in their sexual relations when sanctified by marriage. While man was still sinful merely in having sensuous inclinations, the passionate union of a married couple could be taken as evidence of their participation in God's love. Having this potentiality for holiness, passion had only to emancipate itself of the Christian dogmas in order to be idealized on its own.

The liberation of the passionate occurs in the romanticism of the eighteenth and nineteenth centuries. Love then *becomes* God, working miracles through its sheer emotionality. Romantic love defines itself either exclusively as passion or else as the passionate completion of sensuous interests that would be base and even despicable without it. For its part, the sensuous was also liberating itself. In the seventeenth and eighteenth centuries it successfully rebelled against all religious or edifying categories. Though sometimes violent in its rejection of restraints imposed by both the Reformation and the Counter-Reformation, the sensuous cause—as in Montaigne and Rabelais—had only to return to the medieval belief in the fundamental goodness of sexual pleasure. Being merely the contact between two epidermises, as Sébastien Chamfort called it, sexuality pertained to the class of innocent appetites—like a taste for mutton or a penchant for lovely colors. If sex inspired strong emotions, so much the worse. For what breaks through the skin can always be painful. Better to limit oneself to pleasures that could be controlled and easily modified, and in sexuality these are always sensuous.

In subordinating the sensuous to the passionate, or even eliminating the sensuous entirely as in the romantic puritanism of Rousseau, the nineteenth century wrapped sexuality in an aura of mystery. At one and the same time, it was the holiest and the most forbidding of human activities. Sexual love purified and ennobled mankind, and yet sex was the one area in which curiosity —and even scientific investigation—could not be tolerated. Novels, dramas, operas, and even the ballet seemed to concern themselves with nothing but the terrors and the joys of passion, but without the physical union or sensuous interest that accompanies sexuality in the real world. One can see and hear the passion of Tristan and Isolde, but one can hardly imagine these Wagnerian characters *making love*. In them, as in many products of latter-day romanticism, passion exists at such a distance from the physical possibilities of sex that it can only appear as a ritual that transcends ordinary experience. It once again becomes a part of religion, though now a fanciful and fictionalized religion, instead of being a part of life.

In a young and healthy organism, passion would not depend upon frustration: between each consummation it would swell as sexual needs increased. But in all organisms, passion can be made to flourish as a result of frustration. With its puristic morality, its Victorian restraints, and its extraordinary sense of decorum, the nineteenth century constantly frustrated sensuous impulses and thus augmented the passionate. It is almost as if frustration was increased *for the sake of* creating more and greater passion. In any event, that was the consequence, and quite clearly it was the passionate life—often but not always spiritualized—that the age valued more than anything else.

Thus far, the twentieth century has largely been a flight away from passion. To us in the 1970s it is difficult (though not impossible) to take the tragedy of Tristan and Isolde at its face value. We have found easier, and more delightful, ways of satisfying our sexual needs: sensuous ways based upon a free acquaintance with the body rather than a numinous secrecy that magnifies its emotional importance. With its open tolerance of all and every kind of sex, it is easy to see the contemporary world as a return to the swinging eighteenth century. But the experience of romanticism is not that easily forgotten, and in the present-day acceptance of the sensuous we may be closer to a wholesome reconciliation than at any time in the past.

Without the sensuous, sexual experience would not be the kind of enjoyment that it is for human beings. It would be the expression of burning desire, a gnawing tension, a savage hunger that came upon people for reasons too deep to fathom—an emotional occasion driven by psychological and physiological causes that may hardly enter into consciousness. Without the passionate, sexual experience might be enjoyable enough but not especially meaningful or imperious. It would be calm, relaxing, delectable, and quieting to the nerves though also affording moments of exquisite, even excruciating, pleasure. The sensuous aspect of human sexuality must surely approximate what monkeys and apes enjoy while being groomed by one another. To western man the sensuous has often seemed passive, unworthy of his questing spirit. Like Odysseus in the land of the lotus-eaters, he feels threatened by the tranquillizing effect of mere sensuousness, and by the fact that getting something directly through the senses is rarely as exciting as yearning for it in erotic imagination. This applies to the ancients as well as the moderns. We are not surprised to hear Byron say that "passion is the element in which we live: without it we but vegetate"; [2] but even Plutarch approvingly reports that Lycurgus recommended continence in newly wedded Spartans because "it continued in both parties a still burning love and a new desire of the one to the other." [3]

Neither Lycurgus nor Plutarch believed that passion is "the element in which we live," that it defines the normal or proper function of sexuality. Yet they realized that intimacy seems more valuable to husband and wife when they desire each other ardently. The passionate always runs the risk of being painful or mad; but it contributes a sense of importance that cannot come from the sensuous alone. For its part, the sensuous provides a taste for beauty and pervasive pleasure. Though it often seems mindless and superficial, it satisfies a network of appetites as surely as food or drink.

In sexual experience, the sensuous functions in two ways. First, it is an extremely effective means of awakening libidinal interest. It arouses the male or female, stimulates their desire for one another, and brings the genitals into that condition of excitement which is necessary for their satisfactory operation. In men the visual and auditory senses are highly developed as an agency of sensuousness. That erotic scopophilia, love of looking, which characterizes the human male serves as an anticipatory response to sexual possibilities. Whether he is sitting at a café, waiting for a train, walking through a shop, looking at a painting, or watching a movie, the male uses his eyes for visual consummations which are clearly sexual even if they do not lead to orgasm. Compared to men, women are less often stimulated by sensations of sight or hearing; they tend to rely more on direct physical contact. In both men and women, though especially in women, the tactile sense facilitates like nothing else that experience which is itself what D. H. Lawrence called "the closest touch of all." Directly or indirectly, proximately or at a distance, these sensuous acuities create the appetite for sexual experience. And within the experience itself, foreplay intensifies desire merely by means of the sensuous. Looking, touching, tasting, hearing, smelling—each in accordance with individual preference and momentary inclination —brings about a heightening of interest in the other person and in his sexual availability. Without sensuous foreplay, coitus might occur in ways that could certainly propagate the species. But unless there were some prelude of this sort, however brief or limited, sexual intercourse would hardly be pleasurable for either male or female.

It is this pleasurability that indicates the second function of the sensuous. Quite apart from its capacity to awaken appetite, the sensuous is simply enjoyable in itself. The man who watches a woman undress may do so as a means of stimulating himself; but more often, he takes pleasure in the somewhat passive experience of looking. The naked body, when it is handsome or suggestive, is a delightful thing to see. Seeing it need not necessarily lead on to anything else. It would be a pity to live with nothing but the sexual pleasures of looking, seeing, watching. But one does not have to justify such interests by citing another activity or experience to which they lead. Their justification consists in their inherent enjoyability as purely sensuous moments, and not as mere instrumentalities. In coitus itself, the sensuous does more than just arouse appetites. It also has its own way of satisfying them. The tensions that sensuous foreplay creates issue into orgasmic release which may itself be a function of the sensory excitation rather than a passionate drive or any vehement need for explosive end-pleasure. Though the orgasm is often felt as a response that convulses the entire organism, its pleasures are also localized in genital sensations and sometimes these are not accompanied by strong emotions. In the passionate mode, orgasms tend to be emotionally very powerful. But even so, they may not be more satisfying, and often they are less enjoyable, than the pleasures of the sensuous. And that is why some people are willing to forego the passionate for the sake of sensuous consummations that are easier to attain or more desirable under the circumstances.

For many people, however, sexual behavior would not be satisfying unless it also involved the kind of emotional discharge that the passionate provides. The sensuous then operates not only to stimulate desire and to create pleasures that come from its arousal, but also to direct libidinal interests towards a final release that takes them beyond sensation. Without the mediation of the senses, people would not exist for one another. But their *affinity* to each other is more than merely sensory. Human beings gravitate within each other's sexual orbit through an urgency and compulsion that cannot be explained in terms of sight or touch or any other sense modality. This mutual craving is a need for release resulting from tensions that are partly organic and partly interpersonal. Yearning becomes stronger as the tensions build up; if they are not released enjoyably, yearning can change into anger and hatred. And since frustration and orgasmic failure are always possible, the tensions may be accompanied by fear long before their release is even feasible. In the male, this often results in impotence; in the female, in a thwarting of desire that makes it difficult for her to be sexually aroused. In either event, passion disappears and tends to undermine the sensuous as well. But often they strengthen one another. The sensuous induces sensory awareness, which may then be experienced as a passionate yearning; the passionate impels the sexes into each other, and this may lead to sensory gratification as well as emotional ecstasy. Insofar as they define different attitudes, the sensuous and the passionate are separable from one another; and to some extent, each attitude can often survive without the other. How they may be harmonized, and whether they need to be, is one of the major problems to which this book will continually return.

Since the two modes of sexuality interweave so massively, one may well wonder how it is *possible* for them to separate and even conflict. One feels that left to itself sexual experience would naturally bring about their harmony and joint cooperation. But sexuality cannot be left to itself; it does not exist apart from the rest of human reality. Man differs from all other animals, even the nonhuman primates, in the extent to which his sexual responsiveness pervades each moment and every aspect of his being. As a result, sex frequently conflicts with other interests. It is a threat to many economic, political, and spiritual aspirations whose goals are not always consistent with either erotic element. Civilization in general has evolved as a complex of institutions that often control the sexual for the sake of other ends. This is not to say that civilization must be repressive. It can further each of the modes of sexuality, and in some respects it always has. Moreover, the conflict between sensuous and passionate may not be entirely related to social repressiveness. Even if society were to devote itself to the harmonization of the two aspects, and to the fullest expression of each, there may be something in sexuality itself that could always renew their internal warfare. Let us consider what that might be, and whether it is related to what Freud called "organic repression."

If it were easy to harmonize the sensuous and the passionate, many of the problems of sexuality would quickly disappear. But the fact that whole ideologies have been constructed out of the need to separate the two, and out of the desire to favor one rather than the other, indicates that something very profound impedes a satisfactory harmonization. In his pervasive pessimism about sexual happiness, Freud often stressed the difficulties in satisfying the two modes of sexuality. Discussing the relationship between freedom and total satisfaction, he remarks that not only repression is injurious to human beings but also unrestrained sexual liberty. He then says:

> It is easy to show that the value the mind sets on erotic needs instantly sinks as soon as satisfaction becomes readily obtainable. Some obstacle is necessary to swell the tide of the libido to its height; and at all periods of history, wherever natural barriers in the way of satisfaction have not sufficed, mankind has erected conventional ones in order to be able to enjoy love. This is true both of individuals and of nations. In times during which no obstacles to sexual satisfaction existed, such as, may be, during the decline of the civilizations of antiquity, love became worthless, life became empty, and strong reaction-formations were necessary before the indispensable emotional value of love could be recovered. In this context it may be stated that the ascetic tendency of Christianity had the effect of raising the psychical value of love in a way that the heathen antiquity could never achieve; it developed greatest significance in the lives of the ascetic monks, which were almost entirely occupied with struggles against libidinous temptation.[4]

The obstacles to which Freud refers are the usual repressive devices that tend to increase passion. In saying that they are needed for the "indispensable emotional value of love" and "to swell the tide of the libido to its height," he would *seem* to be arguing for the desirability of the passionate as well as the sensuous. But Freud's argument implies that they cannot both be satisfied. If erotic experience is readily attainable, the sensuous can be gratified; but then—Freud assures us—passion disappears and sexuality ceases to be valuable. Without the barriers of frustration and restraint, love becomes "worthless." For it to recover its emotional importance, sexuality has to defeat its own ends as in the extreme case of Christian asceticism. When that happens, however, the pleasures of the sensuous are also denied. By choosing lesser obstacles to satisfaction, Freud might have envisaged a condition in which some passion, at least, would be compatible with sensuous pleasure. But in this place, he sounds as if the mere fact of being "readily available" deprives sexual experience of its value in either mode.

Freud's argument is plausible from the point of view of those who identify love with passion and think that passion can only originate through obstacles. For if this were true, love would lose its value once the obstacles that create passion have been removed. Like many another raised in the nineteenth century, Freud states more than once that a woman can expect to lose her lover on the very day that she takes him as her husband. He obviously means a lover not in the sense of one who *loves* the woman, but rather in the sense of passionate sexual desire. To those who believe in the sensuous, it will seem strange that sexual love should thus be defined in terms of passion alone. Through the intimacy that marriage affords, lovers can have access to more extensive sensuous pleasure than could ever have been available at a distance. Having overcome the obstacles that separated them, they may enjoy the pleasures of the senses with greater security, greater leisure, and greater likelihood of success. Provided, of course, that sensuousness is valued in itself. If so, the love that *it* defines can never be worthless to those who enjoy the sensuous with utter freedom.

But while Freud neglects the goodness of purely sensuous love, he is not an advocate of passion either. From the paragraph I just quoted, one might have thought he would be. Reared in the romantic tradition, he nevertheless turns against it as one of its most profound critics. In many places he seems horrified at the turmoil and emotional stress that passion involves. Though erotic needs sink in value once obstacles are removed, Freud is sensitive to the way in which the obstacles lead to neurosis and sexual misery. In this respect, he closely resembles Lucretius, who also thought that the power and importance of passion resulted from the frustration of erotic impulses, and who also recommended the regularity of marriage as a means of *eliminating* passion. To both Freud and Lucretius, romantic love is not really valuable: it is only valued, or overvalued, by the passionate interest itself. This has the effect of swelling the tide of the libido, but that has so many unfortunate consequences that neither Lucretius nor Freud thinks that it can lead to sexual happiness.

At other times, however, Freud seemed to hold views of a totally different sort. Together with his pessimism, and even negativism, one also finds indications that possibly he did believe in some kind of harmony between the sensuous and the passionate. When he lists the ingredients in a happy marriage, or what he calls the "completely normal attitude" towards sex, he names the elements of *Sinnlichkeit* and *Zärtlichkeit*.[5] The latter is tenderness or affection. The former his translators render as "sensuality"; but since Freud uses the word with no pejorative intention, I think my term "sensuousness" is more appropriate. The question now arises: Does the fusion of *Sinnlichkeit* and *Zärtlichkeit* also include the passionate?

Freud was not writing with my distinction in mind, and one cannot hope to answer such a question too precisely. But in describing what he considers to be normal sexuality, Freud cites obstacles to final satisfaction which would necessarily seem to foster the passionate throughout maturity. Tracing the libido to infantile demands upon the parents which are unrealistic as well as unsatisfiable, he remarks that adult sexuality is inherently imperfect, inherently incapable of being fully satisfied. Whether this results from organic repression he does not say, but he does refer to universal incest-taboos as the cause of childhood yearnings which inevitably linger on in the adult libido. If this is so, the structure of all sexual love would seem to create passion within itself. To the extent that the beloved is always and necessarily an imago of a parental figure—as Freud insists—a sensuous interest *must* be accompanied by some degree of passionate longing for an unobtainable object. This in turn could prevent even sexual experience that was readily attainable from losing value or becoming wholly worthless.

Given his belief in parental imagoes and their effect upon the emotions, it seems likely that Freud did mean to include the passionate as well as the sensuous in the sexuality of a happy marriage. Discussing the merging of *Sinnlichkeit* and *Zärtlichkeit*, he says that the libidinal objects of maturity "will still be chosen on the model (imago) of the infantile ones, but in the course of time they will attract to themselves the affection that was tied to the earlier ones. A man shall leave his father and his mother—according to the biblical command—and shall cleave unto his wife; affection and sensuality are then united. The greatest intensity of sensual passion ["*sinnlicher Verliebtheit*"] will bring with it the highest psychical valuation of the object—this being the normal overvaluation of the sexual object on the part of a man." [6]

In speaking of "overvaluation," Freud confuses us again. For he uses that term throughout his writings to signify an unwarranted expenditure of libido. It is the dangerous and unrealistic element in all romantic excitement; it is the madness in the condition known as "falling in love." When Freud condemns passion, he does so because he thinks it always leads to overvaluation.[*] Nevertheless, what Freud says in this place would definitely imply that normal sexuality satisfies both the sensuous *and* the passionate by choosing an object which reawakens childhood needs while also being readily accessible. And perhaps it is this theme that we ought to emphasize in his writings. Far from leading us to assume that the sensuous and the passionate are necessarily antagonistic, his argument would then encourage us to try to find the circumstances in which they cooperate. Despite his ambiguities, I think that was Freud's intention. But he did not carry it out, and our age will have to discover new ways of doing so.

It is too early in the development of the life sciences for us to resolve the difficulties we have been examining. But I would like to walk about them a little longer, to understand them better before the following chapters reformulate them in terms of various sexological problems.

I begin, or begin again, by asserting that the sensuous attitude is basically innocent. It is just a playful enjoyment of the body, and of the human personality as it expresses itself through the senses. The sensuous is an aesthetic interest whose materials are sensations related to the genitals and other erotogenic zones.

---

[*] I have discussed this at greater length in my chapter on Freud in *The Nature of Love* (New York, Random House, 1966).

Whether its pleasures lead to orgasm or not, whether it limits itself to foreplay or goes beyond, whether it is experienced with a single partner or many at once, whether it is heterosexual or homosexual, whether it employs the mouth, the anus, the vagina, or any other orifice of the body, it can be approached as an artistic activity designed to maximize and prolong human pleasure. When Ovid speaks of the "art of love," he principally has in mind this aspect of sexuality. And as savages have often been idealized as living at the level of mere sensation, the sensuous is frequently represented by an idyllic image of man in nature. Thus, Stendhal —who distinguishes between sensuous love, passionate love, vanity love, and sympathy love—describes *l'amour sensuel* as an erotic extension of the hunt: "Whilst out shooting, to meet a fresh, pretty country girl who darts away into a wood. Everyone knows the love founded on pleasures of this kind: however unromantic and wretched one's character, it is there that one starts at the age of sixteen." [7] In the visual arts, we often encounter a similar scene—Boucher and Fragonard have captured it to perfection.

Stendhal himself wishes to transcend the sensuous in the direction of the passionate. But nowhere does he insist upon a necessary conflict between the two. And though his entire book on love is devoted to the possibilities of passion love, he also recognizes that it can sometimes be harmful in thwarting man's sensuous nature. In the chapter entitled "Failures" in *De l'Amour*, he shows how the passionate attitude can lead to male impotence resulting from a fear of performance, thereby robbing the lovers of sensory pleasure. And despite his faith in passion as such, Stendhal continually makes remarks such as this one: "Some virtuous and affectionate women have almost no idea at all of sensuous pleasure; they have only very rarely laid themselves open to it, if I may put it so, and even then the raptures of passion love have almost made them forget the pleasures of the body." [8] When he discusses the birth of love, Stendhal gives the sensuous at least as much importance as the passionate: "To love is to derive pleasure from seeing, touching, and feeling through all one's senses and as closely as possible, a lovable person who loves us." [9]

Stendhal does not take the defense of the sensuous any further; and in his novels, its role and its significance are always tantalizingly unclear. But in seeking to harmonize it with passion love, he accords the sensuous a dignity that many of his contemporaries found shocking. In eastern philosophy this dignity has often turned into spiritual idealization, the sensuous being refined into a method for *extirpating* man's passionate cravings. In the sexual yoga of Hinduism, Buddhism, and Taoism, male and female bodies achieve spiritual oneness through a spontaneous and unforced sharing of sensory pleasures. Intercourse occurs not through any action or doing, not because of any "grasping desire," but rather as a passionless enjoyment of contemplative love: "One finds out what it can mean simply to look at the other person, to touch hands, or to listen to the voice. If these contacts are not regarded as leading to something else, but rather allowed to come to one's consciousness as if the source of activity lay in them and not in the will, they become sensations of immense subtlety and richness." [10]

In recommending the sensuous as they do, the eastern philosophers have one thing in common with western hedonists like Ovid. As in much erotic literature both eastern and western, they strengthen the sensuous approach by making sexual experience routine and even casual—though also very sophisticated in the ways of maximizing pleasure. But easygoing sex is rarely cathartic; and cleverness in the use of the body need not lead to powerful emotions. Can anyone following minute instructions about positions and techniques, of the sort to be found in the *Kama Sutra* for instance, really get carried away by an ardent longing for the beloved? Lovemaking can be taught, but not passion itself. The same applies to much of contemporary sexology. Readers of the works of Masters and Johnson may learn a great deal that can liberate their propensity to sensuous pleasure. But in their attempt to make sexuality less mysterious, less inhibited, and also less frightening, such studies do nothing to facilitate the passionate response. Perhaps that is why the therapeutic advice that has issued from this research seems to minimize the desirability of passion. In their book on sexual inadequacy, Masters and Johnson caution against that "pattern of demanding pelvic thrusting" in which passion generally manifests itself: "The wife repeatedly must be assured that this forceful approach will not contribute to facility of response. If the husband initiates the driving, thrusting coital pattern, the wife must devote conscious effort to accommodate to the rhythm of his thrusting, and her opportunity for quiet sensate pleasure in coital connection is lost." [11] This emphasis upon "sensate focus," and in general the sensuous attitude, may be interpreted as merely therapeutic; but as we shall see throughout this book, there may be no way of differentiating between therapeutic means and permanent conditioning in Masters' and Johnson's approach to sexual possibilities.

Since passion so often originates in pathology, one may not want to increase it on many occasions. To do so, however, involves something more than a concern for sensuous techniques. It requires a *yearning* for the person one is with, a *craving* to penetrate her and to be penetrated by him, a *striving* for the deepest contact, a *need* for emotional union that enables each to participate in the other, to appropriate the other, and possibly to give oneself as well.

Whence arises this passionate need that people often have for one another, and that they express in sexuality? From person to person it varies greatly. Some theorists even postulate a fixed quantity with which an individual is endowed. If this were the case, passion would be an emotional constant for each person, analogous to temperament or musical talent or mathematical genius. As there are volatile spirits and others that are more sedate, so too would there be human beings fundamentally more or less passionate than others. At the same time, however, we know that sexual passion is correlated with physiological maturation. In people who are repressed at least to the extent characteristic of the western world, passion extends from adolescence into middle age. The time span varies greatly, but most young people go through a period of passionate potential that eventually becomes kinetic in relation to at least one erotic object. Through the middle years passion tends to diminish, though the onset of menopause makes the decline more noticeable in women than in men. In both sexes the trend often reverses itself in the late thirties, the forties, or even the fifties, with an outburst of passional interest that some people call the middle-age adolescence. As if to compensate for the gradual loss of emotional capability, nature gives men and women another chance to feel towards some beloved that youthful turmoil which everyone cherishes but no one manages properly when it first appears.

Fictional literature often centers about the vicissitudes of human experience at these two periods in a person's life. They set the biological time for tragedy as well as comedy. One would have difficulty understanding *Phaedra* in any of its versions unless one realized that the heroine has reached the time of sudden recrudescence in passion that many women experience as they approach the menopause. On the other hand, the dilemma that Shaw's doctor undergoes in *The Doctor's Dilemma* would not exist if Ridgeon were ten years younger or ten years older. Having reached the age of forty in a somewhat celibate condition, Ridgeon complains of a curious and unlocalized "aching." Sir Patrick, his older colleague, diagnoses the ailment quite correctly: "It's very common between the ages of seventeen and twenty-two. It sometimes comes on again at forty or thereabouts. You're a bachelor, you see. It's not serious—if you're careful." [12]

Though geared to physiological developments common to the species, these temporal factors are also a function of social and psychological determinants. Some people never fall in love, others seem to do so all the time. Furthermore, the state of passionate desire is so highly prized by men and women in the western world that a great deal of effort goes into trying to awaken or reawaken it throughout the years of maturity. What came so easily in early youth has to be carefully cultivated later on. Even in first love, however, passion is obviously psychogenic to a considerable degree. Theodor Reik has argued that passionate love arises as part of the adolescent's attempt to fulfill some ego ideal. Having been frustrated in our striving for self-perfection, he says, we transfer the image of this ideal to another person. Since no one can *really* provide the perfection we crave, love must always be illusory: "All love is founded on a dissatisfaction with oneself. It is an attempt to escape from oneself in search of a better, an ideal self. The lover imagines that he has found it in his object. Is love thus an illusion? Of course it is. . . ." [13] Romantic love or the state of falling in love would thus differ from other love only in its emotional intensity. Its passional ferocity Reik explains as an effort, a desperate effort, to rescue a menaced ego through the attempt to appropriate that perfect goodness promised by one's illusory image of the beloved.

I have elsewhere* suggested that, even at its most ardent, love is not necessarily an illusion. But Reik is also wrong in thinking that dissatisfaction accounts for passion. Strong sexual impulse is part of the sheer human vitality that *everyone* prizes, not merely those who are dissatisfied with themselves. Passionate desire is not greater in those who are more dissatisfied with themselves, or diminished in those who are less dissatisfied. It is true that passion implies a compelling need. Unless one wants the woman or man, this particular woman or man on this particular occasion, one will not feel a passionate drive. But to say this is not to say that there is a perfection which we lack and which causes us to be dissatisfied with ourselves and which we hope to attain by possessing the woman or the man. What we lack is precisely the state of oneness with this other person which we achieve by means of our passion. Making love is more than just the removing of a dissatisfaction. It can also be an emergent condition, an emotional unity, desirable in itself and not as the mere remedy for a menaced ego. The ego may feel menaced if it has no passionate desires; but passion does not arise—except in pathological cases—as a device for escaping prior failures in oneself.

It is passion which enables us to *care* about other people, to want them and to want to be wanted by them. It provides that vital urgency without which we could not identify with fellow creatures struggling like ourselves in a world we never made. It overcomes loneliness and isolation by making us yearn to be with other men and women. If we had no such feeling, could they be persons who matter to us? Could we be persons for them as well? The answers to these questions may be affirmative since the sensuous mode creates its own social joys—friendly consummations which are often gentler and more pacific than those that result from the passionate. But without the impetus of passion, a purely sensuous society could not mould those affective bonds which ordinarily belong to the very concept of a person.

* In Part I of *The Nature of Love*.

Since the beginning of time, human beings have always sought means of increasing passional desire in one another and in themselves. One could write a history of mankind by reference to love potions alone. Even those who idealize the sensuous recognize the importance that passion has for most people. In his book on the physiology of marriage, Balzac defines love as "the poetry of the senses"; yet he constantly reminds us that even sensory pleasure deteriorates unless passion is also aroused. In the western world men have generally sought to awaken desire in the female by their status in society, whereas women were expected to increase the male's libidinal interest through the beauty of their face and figure. Liberated women who nowadays complain that men have used them as physical contrivances are right to protest against such treatment. But they will never understand the condition unless they realize that these roles have existed partly because women saw no other way of increasing masculine desire. In the rudimentary sex act the female does not need to get anything ready, while the man must have an erection. And this is more likely to occur if the man feels secure and even admirable. For reasons of their own, sometimes good and sometimes bad, women (not all women, but many) have been willing to submit to almost anything that will create this feeling in the male—and thereby augment his ardor for the female.

As a symbol of this sociobiological relationship, one need only consider the institution of the dancing-girl or striptease artist. With his greater sexual interest in visual sensations, the male enjoys the exhibition of female flesh more than the female enjoys the exhibition of male flesh. In all societies women have regularly provided such enjoyment. In doing so, however, the self-exhibiting female systematically hides as much as she reveals. She causes frustration through her teasing and evasive movements, through the repressive suggestion that there is something naughty or forbidden in the presentation of her nudity, and through the distance that her performance imposes upon the male who can watch but cannot touch her. Frustration of this sort may challenge a man but it does not threaten him. The performance is itself a means of flattering his sexual interests. It arouses desire, and sometimes passion, in the male.

Dancing-girls and stripteasers make up a tiny percentage of the female population. Moreover, they are relegated to the lower classes as a way of assuring men that the male is ultimately superior to the female despite her sexual powers. Nevertheless, the dancing-girl represents all women inasmuch as she specializes in arousing masculine desire through the use of her body, and that is one of the principal roles which western society has demanded of women in general. The equivalent among men—crooners, movie idols, and others who devote themselves to arousing women—have no comparable importance. They do not represent attitudes expected of men as a whole. On the contrary, those who excite women merely by entertaining them have generally been scorned by other men, or even hounded by society as in the Don Juan myth. Men want women to be passionate, but only when they admire masculine achievements that belong to the world of men and that men themselves respect. The male entertainer does not live in that world, at least not in the way that the politician, the soldier, and the football player do. To some extent, this phenomenon is culturally determined. To some extent, however, it is related to the fact that women often fear the consequences of their passion and will yield to its ecstatic abandon only when they feel protected by a vigorous and masterful male. Don Juan seduces them by pretending to be that kind of man. When they realize he is not, they turn on him with all the fury that passion has created in them.

As Freud suggests in that passage I quoted earlier, natural barriers and artificial obstacles tend to increase passion and magnify its value. In the western world the tradition that stems from Plato sets up obstacles by means of the very idealizations that structure its attitudes towards love. Plato defines eros as the desire for the Good; but then he tells us that the Good is unattainable in experience. All human desire must therefore be a striving after perfection which is both hopeless and inescapable. If one could really *live* this philosophy, one's life would be a throbbing passion from beginning to end. That being impossible, courtly and romantic love make lesser arrangements among mere human beings. Like Platonism, they augment the passionate by means of alternate inducements and repressions not wholly different from the striptease. The medieval lady was revered as the visible exemplar of beauty but always worshiped from afar, accessible to the poetic imagination but never to be touched or enjoyed through carnal intercourse. In the nineteenth century, the courtly concepts were universalized so that *every* woman could become an angel in the household. She was to shine forth as the image of a perfect goodness men desired without herself being subject to passions that might have quieted the endless yearnings of her husband. Her theoretical lack of sexual interest served as a final and limiting obstacle that men could use to maximize their own passion. Whenever the authentic feelings—sensuous *or* passionate—of a normally sexual woman burst through the conventional barriers, she was made to feel guilty or sick. Only in our century has society come to recognize that the lustful woman is not abnormal, certainly no more so than the lustful male.

In our day the women's liberation movement, and in general the toughness of the female, may provide (may even be *designed* to provide) a new enticement to the male. In their professed belligerence women may be changing tactics but not the strategy; as in Aristophanes' *Lysistrata*, they get what they want by frustrating men as women always have. But times *do* change. If some liberationists rebel against all heterosexual possibilities, perhaps it is because they do not realize that the major battle has been won. Women are now free to enjoy sexual experience in any way they can. And so are men. The old barriers no longer exist. We shall have to find more positive ways of making sex intense and meaningful as well as delectable.

In making this attempt, we may begin by recognizing that Plato was right to associate passion with a search for ideals. Though the Good is too abstract a notion to be of much use, it may very well be the case that without standards of value the phenomenon of passion could not exist. The passionate is not wholly reducible to the drive for coitus, or even the need for orgasmic consummation. These may serve as characteristic ingredients of sexual passion, but they themselves presuppose a craving to unite and a feeling that it is *important* to do so. Passion would not arise unless the desired person, or the activity of uniting, or both, were cherished by the lover as something *worthy* of his desire. As a basis for this valuation, there may be any number of biological, psychological, and sociological causes. But they are not always the same, and no one of them is either necessary or sufficient. There must be something in valuation itself which engenders the passionate. I have suggested that in a healthy organism passion arises spontaneously during the years of sexual maturity, and therefore that it is not entirely a function of artificial barriers. If this is true, perhaps it results from the fact that healthy organisms create standards of value as part of their response to reality. Far from being artificial, the social restraints that increase passion may often derive from a pervasive need to create values.

These are merely speculations, however, and will remain so until they can be verified by the empirical sciences. In the following chapters we shall be studying various problems in the theory of sex which are both empirical and philosophical. They are all related to the conflict between the sensuous and the passionate; and they all involve ambiguities in the use of terms like "libido," "drive," "desire," "consummation," "orgasm," and even "sex." In the male and in the female, the sensuous and the passionate express themselves through different behavioral dispositions and different orgasmic consummations that need to be delineated with as much precision as science can presently afford. If the passionate is "natural" in the sense of being more than just a product of artificial barriers, one must determine what its natural condition may be. And since the sensuous and the passionate conflict in so much of human experience, one must consider ways in which they may be harmonized. It is also possible that harmonization is not desirable, or even feasible, for all people on all occasions. In formulating a pluralistic approach to sexological problems, we cannot assume that any one solution is necessarily the right one for all the situations that constitute human experience.

Chapter 3

TYPES OF FEMALE ORGASM

Since erotic consummations are so diverse among themselves, many people have wondered whether orgasms are basically alike or whether they can be analyzed into different types. In the male, problems about orgasm are related to the nature of ejaculation and the circumstances under which it occurs. In the female, the criteria for orgasm are less obvious. Recent writers often employ what is virtually an arbitrary definition of the term and then assume that others always mean the same. The result has been a great deal of vagueness and unnecessary confusion. As a way of approaching the problem, this chapter will seek to reawaken a controversy which was only temporarily laid to rest by the laboratory research of the 1960s. The issue is whether or not convulsive contractions in the muscles of the outer third of the vagina, or in general those forming the pelvic floor, are a necessary element in the female orgasm. As I mentioned in an earlier chapter, these contractions are taken by some sexologists to be an essential criterion for the existence of orgasm. In the reports of other researchers, such as the one by Elkan from which I have already quoted, one occasionally finds evidence to indicate that not all orgasms conform to this criterion. Examining this controversy will enable us to formulate an analysis of different types of female orgasm. In later chapters we can use this analysis to resolve problems related to various questions about female sexuality.

The most succinct statement of the controversy occurs in the Levine-Malleson exchange in 1948, published under the heading, "A criterion for orgasm in the female." In routine history-taking at the Margaret Sanger Research Bureau, Dr. Lena Levine noticed that some women attain "satisfaction and resulting complete relaxation with no description of involuntary, perineal contractions." [1] Levine uses the phrase "perineal contractions" whereas Malleson (as we shall soon see) prefers the term "vulval contractions." They both are referring to contractions in the outer third of the vagina which Masters and Johnson refer to as "contractions of the orgasmic platform." In this book, I shall use "vulval contractions" interchangeably with "contractions of the orgasmic platform."

In describing her observations, Levine goes on to say:

The description of the general reaction was so varied and depended so much upon the emotional type and personality of the individual, that it was extremely difficult to make a definite classification of the woman's response. Where the involuntary, perineal contractions occur, they are definite and are observable by the woman, if her attention is directed to them. . . . And once observed, it follows that every time orgasm is reached, the contractions occur. But what about those women who have not experienced these involuntary, muscular contractions and yet who describe an intense general reaction, which seems to reach a peak and then subsides? Our impression is that these women have not really reached a peak but a point in the rise of tension just short of it, with subsequent slow release. That this reaction is satisfactory to the patient, is unquestionable, and the patient can be reassured that this reaction is adequate for her. But it cannot be described as an orgasm. . . . By accepting involuntary, perineal contractions as the criterion for the female orgasm, we would have a definite standard for evaluation of the reaction of the female, which can be used in diagnosis and in treatment. . . . [2]

With respect to orgasms that involve vulval contractions, Masters has pointed out that "irritability, emotional instability, restlessness, pelvic discomfort, lack of sleep" are the usual aftermaths of orgasmic frustration.[3] This being so, it is surprising that Levine should think that women can be excited to a point "just short of" orgasm of this sort and yet find the experience satisfying. But since the patients do report satisfaction which is "intense" and "unquestionable," satisfaction that seems "to reach a peak and then subsides," one wonders by what authority Levine or anyone else can inform these women that they have not *really* had an orgasm. It would seem more plausible to believe that female orgasms are not always the same, in fact that they vary significantly in their behavioral manifestations.

Dr. Joan Malleson, a London gynecologist (1900–1956), explicitly asserts that not all orgasms involve vulval contractions. She replies to Levine's suggestion as follows:

Dr. Levine writes as though the observable contractions at the vulva (not confusing voluntary ones which could be simulated) is a proof of orgasm. It is only a proof of clitoral orgasm, but even then, that must not be taken as being proof of satisfactory clitoral orgasm. Women can have this and experience no satisfaction whatever; it is the exact equivalent of the male who has an emission without erection. It is most important, I consider, that false criteria of this sort should not be accepted.

I wish I could be more specific about vaginal orgasm. I do not myself believe that there are "measurements" that can be observed *always*, and assessed; and I do not think that these vulval contractions are necessarily found with a true vaginal orgasm. Such movement as there is, I should say, is confined much more to the levator and the upper vaginal musculature. . . .

I certainly have one patient, who had an unsuccessful analysis, and whose husband is deceived by the fact of these vulval contractions, which are perfectly genuine in her case. She gets them with clitoral orgasm, but the orgasm gives no pleasure whatever, although she is glad to feel that there is some muscular response. This woman has a total vaginal anesthesia, and is certain that she has never had vulval contractions of this sort of any spontaneous nature at any time, other than during clitoral stimulation. But as I say, it is as valueless as ejaculation in the male without an erection.[4] [Her italics.]

Apparently the Masters and Johnson laboratory research of the '60s has not resolved the basic issue since many gynecologists still believe that not all orgasms involve the contractions. Eustace Chesser, for example, writing in 1969, states:

Another popular fallacy is that an orgasm is not real without powerful contractions of the vagina. Those women who do not experience these contractions worry about their inability to attain orgasm. They vainly pursue an imaginary ideal. When closely questioned they admit they find intercourse intensely enjoyable. They have, in fact, experienced the release from tension which is what constitutes orgasm. All they miss are certain aftereffects which do not necessarily add to the pleasure because they happen to be so striking.[5]

Prior to Chesser, Kinsey had also distinguished between the orgasm and its aftereffects: ". . . explosive discharge of neuromuscular tensions at the peak of sexual response is what we identify as orgasm. The spasms into which the individual is thrown as a result of that release, we consider the aftereffects of that orgasm."[6] In talking of spasms in general, Kinsey says only that they are "the usual product" of orgasmic release; and with respect to vulval or perineal spasms, he is even more tentative. "Some women" experience them, he says, but it is difficult "to determine whether the lack of vaginal spasms represents any loss of pleasure for a female."[7] At the same time, Kinsey does maintain that "orgasm in the female matches the orgasm of the male in every physiologic detail except for the fact that it occurs without ejaculation."[8] How this can be the case if the female orgasm need not be accompanied by contractions comparable to the male's, Kinsey does not tell us and one can only speculate about the effect of this ambiguity upon the data he collected.

One can see why Masters and Johnson would have sided with Levine. As descendants of the Behaviorist tradition, they were undoubtedly attracted by the fact that contractions of the orgasmic platform *can* be considered "a definite standard." When asked at a symposium for his definition of female orgasm, Masters stated: "For our anatomic and physiologic purposes, if the orgasmic platform contracts, the woman is having an orgasm. This phenomenon happens in the outer third of the vagina."[9] Such contractions are verifiable by the woman herself, by her partner, and by the laboratory scientist. Moreover, these contractions are consistently accompanied by physiological changes such as generalized vasocongestion, increased muscle tension, rhythmic contractions of the uterus, heavy and rapid respiration, increased heart rate, and high blood pressure. Masters and Johnson chose to concentrate upon measuring these and other events which occur in this kind of orgasm and which can be induced in almost all women.

But in focusing on orgasms that *do* involve vulval contractions, Masters and Johnson have neglected every other kind of climax which many women would be likely to call an "orgasm." Should a woman turn to Masters and Johnson for enlightenment, they can, by means of a vibrator if all else fails, show her what "the" orgasm is supposed to be. But more often, women who are truly satisfied by a habit of climactic release from tension *without* the contractions do not present themselves for clinical counseling. Thus it is easy for sexologists to ignore their type of sexuality.

Paul J. Fink, in a study which tries to resolve some of the differences between the Freudians and Masters and Johnson, reports that

> Masters has collected a large amount of psychological information from his subjects. For instance, he has indicated that some women may show an intense vaginal response in orgasm from masturbatory activity only to report that subjectively it was not very exciting. In coition, such women may exhibit a minimal orgastic response but may find it exceedingly pleasurable subjectively.[10]

But if an orgasm is a release of sexual tension due to vulval contractions, how can a strong contractile response be less exciting than a minimal one? When a woman finds the lesser response so "exceedingly pleasurable," the reason may well be more than merely "psychological."

This brings up an important methodological point. Women keep talking about the "emotional satisfaction" of the so-called vaginal orgasm.[11] This emotional satisfaction is assumed to be subjective or psychological by Masters and Johnson, and hence outside the realm of physiological investigation. But emotions are not merely mental. They have physiological components, and most of these have been studied by reputable physiologists for many years. If there are emotional differences between different kinds of orgasm, then the physiological differences ought to be measurable. It is possible that some of the emotional aspects of orgasm may disappear when the sex partners know they are being observed in a laboratory. And if this is so, there would be a tendency for all orgasms to look alike despite their normal diversity. The fact that Masters and Johnson never report data from women who distinguish between their own "clitoral" and "vaginal" responses may itself indicate a major limitation in their findings. They seem to ignore a population of women represented by one who wrote the following in a letter to Masters and Johnson: "I just know that if someone would watch me copulate with a partner, the best I could do would be a little outer clitoral climax, as fast as possible to get the silly situation over with. I do not call that an orgasm." [12] What it is that this woman would call an orgasm I do not know, but the quantitative reports now available which *do* distinguish between types of orgasms have been made by a pair of physiologists, C. A. and B. Fox, who assembled laboratory equipment in their own bedroom, thereby avoiding all human observers.[13] Their research will be discussed in the course of this chapter, and also in the Appendix.

With these methodological considerations in mind, we may now reformulate our original question: If a woman can have a highly pleasurable experience with a "minimal orgastic response," might she not have a climactic and wholly satisfying sexual release with *no* vulval contractions whatever? And in such a case, is it not probable that an untutored woman would naturally call such a climax an "orgasm"? Lee Rainwater, the sociologist, complains of the difficulty in ascertaining what women actually mean when they refer to orgasm:

> Women, and their husbands, were asked specifically about whether and how often the wife achieved orgasm (or "came" or reached a "climax" or some other synonym). Most of the respondents understood the question and were able to give a response that sounded reasonable. However, over a third of the

women answered in ways that left the analyst unsure of whether they actually referred to orgasm.[14]

By sorting out the different types of sexual climax, perhaps a certain amount of confusion can be eliminated.

Three new terms will be introduced which, it is hoped, will avoid all normative significance:

(1) The "vulval orgasm" is characterized by involuntary, rhythmic contractions of the orgasmic platform, as well as by the other physiological changes which have been measured in the laboratory by Masters and Johnson, and to which I have already referred. This kind of orgasm does not depend upon coitus since it can be produced by a variety of other procedures, for instance clitoral masturbation. In other words, it may be coital or noncoital.

(2) The "uterine orgasm" does not involve any contractions of the orgasmic platform, but it does involve emotional changes which can be measured. The most notable of these is apnea caused by laryngeal displacement. Apnea is an interruption of breathing, which in this case results from a strong contraction of the cricopharyngeus muscle in the throat. This muscle, which draws the larynx down and back, is linked with the abdominal viscera by a circuit involving the vagus nerve. The crico-pharyngeus muscle tenses under many circumstances, for example sobbing, laughing, yawning, screaming. One can contract it voluntarily by "swallowing" the back of the tongue. In the uterine orgasm its contraction, and the resulting apnea, follow upon a gasping, cumulative type of breathing. After considerable diaphragmatic tension has been achieved, the apnea occurs as an involuntary breath-holding response. The orgasm results when the breath is explosively exhaled; it is immediately succeeded by a feeling of relaxation and sexual satiation. This kind of orgasm occurs in coitus alone, and it largely depends upon the pleasurable effects of uterine and visceral buffeting by the thrusting penis. Subjectively the orgasm is felt to be "deep," i.e., dependent on repeated penis-cervix contact. In the sexological literature, its respiratory and emotional effects

were outlined by Roubaud, whose description of the female orgasm Kinsey much admired, maintaining that it had not been surpassed by later authors: [15]

> In cases of intense exaltation . . . [the breathing may be] temporarily suspended, in consequence of laryngeal spasm, and the air, after being pent up for a time in the lungs, is finally forcibly expelled, and they utter incoherent and incomprehensible words.[16]

(3) The "blended orgasm" combines elements of the previous two kinds. As with the uterine orgasm, it depends upon the female's desire for intromission and is followed by a terminative feeling of satisfaction and fulfillment. It is characterized by contractions of the orgasmic platform, but the orgasm is subjectively regarded as *deeper* than a vulval orgasm. Some women report a sensation of vaginal "heaving" or, as one put it: "My vagina swallows one or two times and I have an orgasm." [17] From the reports to which the present writer has access, apnea would seem always to occur in blended orgasms. It occurs repetitively for about five seconds at a time in the moments preceding the climax.[18] In her description of what is (in effect) the blended orgasm, Robinson says: "With the approach of orgasm the breathing becomes interrupted; inspiration comes in forced gasps and expiration occurs with a heavy collapse of the lungs." [19] The data of the Foxes provide quantitative corroboration of this account.[20]

In giving this analysis, I have intentionally ignored the common distinction between "clitoral orgasm" and "vaginal orgasm." In the next chapter, an attempt will be made to clarify these terms and to see how they have functioned in the history of sexology. Here I need only remark that they have taken on so many confusing and value-laden connotations that surely they ought to be avoided in scientific discourse wherever possible. For one thing, all types of coitus entail *some* clitoral stimulation. As Masters says in an interview: ". . . it is physically impossible *not* to stimulate the clitoris during intercourse. . . . You see, with each thrust the minor labia are pulled down toward the rectum and, in the process, stimulate the shaft of the clitoris." [21] [His italics.] The mere fact of clitoral involvement in no way indicates how or how much the clitoris functions in various orgasms. But since all orgasms are "clitoral" to *some* extent, this terminology is hardly useful for distinguishing one kind from another. For another thing, the term "clitoral orgasm" gives the misleading impression that *only* the clitoris is involved in some orgasmic responses. Prior to Masters and Johnson, Robinson made the following blunder: "The clitoral orgasm takes place on the clitoris only. It excludes the vagina from sensual participation." [22] There is, however, no such thing as an orgasm taking place on the clitoris alone. Even mild or superficial vulval orgasms involve the following muscles: bilateral bulbocavernosi, transverse perineals, external anal sphincter and rectus abdominus, with secondary involvement of the levator ani and the ischiocavernosi. Since these are all muscles in the vulval region, most of which have no direct effect on the clitoris, it is clearly preferable to talk of a vulval rather than a clitoral orgasm. Finally, the words "clitoral orgasm" have acquired a pejorative sense. They have traditionally been used for the sake of contrasting vulval orgasms unfavorably with the more desirable phenomenon called "vaginal orgasm." There is no reason, however, to disparage the vulval orgasm or to consider it inferior. For a variety of sexual opportunities it is optimal and even ideal; many women have no need for anything else.

The term "vaginal orgasm" is worth abandoning not only because it implies a unique superiority which has never been proved, but also because it too has acquired a welter of different meanings. It has been used to signify any of the following: a coital vulval orgasm, called "vaginal" because the penis stimulates the vagina during intercourse even though the response differs in no physiological way from noncoital vulval orgasms; a blended orgasm, sometimes referred to as deep and characterized by an emotional satisfaction which is absent from many vulval orgasms; a uterine orgasm which is both deep and emotionally satisfying. In short, the term has been applied to almost any kind of coital experience that a woman would consider climactic and desirable. It is too ambiguous to be of much use.

The term "uterine orgasm" is problematic in one sense. As

Masters and Johnson show,[23] every vulval orgasm is accompanied by uterine contractions, and therefore to a certain extent all orgasms might be considered "uterine." But it is not the uterine *contractions* which prompt the label, but rather the fact that the uterus is repetitively displaced by the penis, thereby causing stimulation of the peritoneum, a highly sensitive organ. The peritoneum is the membranous lining which surrounds the intestines, uterus, and other abdominal viscera. One may also speculate that the uterus contracts more *strongly* in a uterine orgasm than in others. Heiman writes:

> Observations of large farm animals (mare and cow) indicate that . . . uterine contractions are not only present during mating, but that they start when the female sights the male, increase as the male approaches and mounts, and reach a climax at the ejaculation of the male. Ejaculation is accompanied by tetanic contractions of the uterus.[24]

In tetanic contractions of the uterus the clenching of the womb persists for several seconds—in the case of the cow, sometimes for nearly a minute.[25] If a uterine orgasm is comparable to what a mare or cow experiences, then one would expect it to be accompanied by tetanic contractions. Even if it were, however, the woman undergoing the experience would be oblivious to the tetanic contractions as such. They undoubtedly would *augment* her peritoneal stimulation; but since no woman can be sure what her uterus is doing at the moment of climax, we must leave this measurement for future physiologists. One would especially like to know whether there are different kinds or patterns of uterine contractions, different ways in which the waves of muscular tension and relaxation are coordinated.

If the Fox data are typical, blended orgasms entail a pressure differential within the uterus before and after orgasm in such fashion that the uterus acts like a rubber squeeze-bulb that is first squeezed and then released, enabling the semen to be sucked in and transported towards the Fallopian tubes.[26] It is likely that the uterine suction response measured by the Foxes is also a consistent element in what I am calling the uterine orgasm, but measurements for this phenomenon have not yet been made in the context of the uterine orgasm. The experiments of the Foxes contradict Masters' and Johnson's findings with respect to uterine suction. In the Appendix we shall examine this conflicting evidence in relation to problems about fertility.

Before presenting a more detailed phenomenological description of the uterine orgasm, one should emphasize the fact that involuntary laryngeal displacement is characteristic of a variety of emotions. Grief, surprise, fear, joy—all of these often involve laryngeal displacement with concomitant diaphragmatic tension. This fact may help to explain what some women mean when they describe a "vaginal" orgasm as "nothing but emotion." For example, Doris Lessing in *The Golden Notebook* writes the following:

A vaginal orgasm is emotion and nothing else, felt as emotion and expressed in sensations that are indistinguishable from emotion. The vaginal orgasm is a dissolving in a vague, dark generalized sensation like being swirled in a warm whirlpool.[27]

Lessing contrasts this more satisfying experience with the "sharp violence" of a "clitoral" orgasm.[28] The following description of the uterine orgasm is more precise:

The stimulus is uterine jostling. That is what produces the response. But the response is a kind of laryngeal spasm in the throat, accompanied by tension of the diaphragm. The breath is inhaled cumulatively, each gasp adding to the amount of breath contained previously in the lungs. When the diaphragm is sufficiently tense, the breath is involuntarily held in the lungs, and the crico-pharyngeus muscle tenses, drawing the larynx down and back. The feeling is one of "strangling in ecstasy." Finally the crico-pharyngeus snaps back to a resting position, and the breath, simultaneously, is exhaled. The suddenness with which this occurs produces the explosiveness without which the term "orgasm" would hardly apply. For a day or two following an orgasm, I sense a pronounced tonic state of the deep vaginal muscles. The satisfaction is so complete that subsequent climaxes are quite impossible for at least a day. For me, the relief from sexual tension which this crico-pharyngeal orgasm brings is analogous to the relief from pent-up nervous tension which an acute sobbing spell may bring. Both involve crico-pharyngeal action. Perhaps ethologists would care to know that my facial expressions are different in my two types of orgasm. In a clitoral orgasm, my teeth are bared and my brow is furrowed with "anger" lines. In this other kind of orgasm, my brow is smooth and the corners of my parted lips are drawn back, although my teeth are not bared: i.e., a typical "fear" expression. The significance of this is not clear to me.

Masters and Johnson make no mention whatsoever of any kind of apnea or laryngeal displacement. Indeed there is reason to think that neither of these occurs with the simple hyperventilation typical of a vulval orgasm. Hyperventilation is a heavy, panting type of breathing—generally regular, quite rapid, and free of interruptions. It is characteristic of breathing in the male during coitus, and in fact most males manifest no other pattern of breathing whether or not they are active or passive prior to ejaculation. The Foxes' measurements of breathing patterns in the blended orgasm indicate that, at least for this one woman, repetitive brief apnea is a consistent precursor of her terminative orgasm. Mrs. Fox's normal response is to have two sets of contractions of the orgasmic platform during intercourse. The second, while far more satisfying subjectively, was shown to be less intense according to blood pressure readings. This is in keeping with the psychological reports mentioned earlier of women whose "minimal" coital orgasms are more exciting than preliminary stronger ones.

The blended orgasm's pattern of brief, repetitive apnea, while differing from the panting type of hyperventilation of the vulval orgasm, also differs from the apnea of the uterine orgasm. In a uterine orgasm a cumulative amount of breath is held in the lungs and the apnea may be total for twenty or thirty seconds just prior to the sexual climax. It is not improbable that such prolonged apnea is inconsistent with contractions of the orgasmic platform and that this is why it contributes to a different kind of orgasmic peak. Perhaps the fact that contractions of the orgasmic platform in coitus seem to depend on more or less strenuous pelvic movements by the female may help to explain the incompatibility between the contractions and prolonged apnea. Such activity would very likely cause a woman to become "out of breath," thereby requiring her to inhale periodically and so precluding the possibility of prolonged apnea. In the typical uterine orgasm, the pelvis stays motionless, although muscles in the limbs and face are tensed, as are the diaphragm and the crico-pharyngeus.

Behavioral differences between stimuli leading to the three types of orgasm include the kind of thrusting involved. For a uterine orgasm, the thrusting is strong, accelerating, deep and relatively brief—of the kind which Masters and Johnson would condemn as being too "demanding." [29] Masters and Johnson repeatedly advise men to be gentle and slow in order to elicit the woman's orgasm. The blended orgasm, on the other hand, seems to result from thrusting that starts out slow and then, within three to twenty minutes, becomes strong and deep. (The same timing is also mentioned by Lowen.[30]) That this time period is not statistically normal is indicated by Kinsey's finding that 75 percent of all males in his sample ejaculate within two minutes after intromission.[31] The two-minute period of time—brief as it may seem—is entirely consistent with the requirements of the uterine orgasm; but obviously it is not conducive to vulval and blended orgasms. The question of how long, in minutes, intromission should last is one which Masters and Johnson avoid. To define "premature ejaculation" as they do, in terms of the duration required to elicit vulval contractions, is misleading in view of the fact that some women reach this kind of orgasm either very slowly or never. We shall return to this question in subsequent chapters.

The effect of cervical contact is also relevant, and it too is never formally treated in the Masters and Johnson study. This is surprising, since Kinsey is clear on this point:

> [The cervix] has been identified by some of our subjects, as well as by many of the patients who go to gynecologists, as an area which must be stimulated by the penetrating male organ before they can achieve full and complete satisfaction in orgasm.[32]

> Many females, and perhaps a majority of them, find that when coitus involves deep vaginal penetrations, they secure a type of satisfaction which differs from that provided by the stimulation of the labia or clitoris alone.[33]

Recently LeMon Clark's experiments give substance to the reports of these women.[34] He had women stimulate themselves first with a clitoral vibrator alone, and subsequently with two vibrators at once, one giving a continuous, mild jostling to the uterus, and the other providing the usual clitoral stimulation. Nearly all of his subjects reported far greater satisfaction resulting from the simultaneous joint stimulation. Clark suggests that the enhanced satisfaction results from pleasurable peritoneal stimulation. If this hypothesis is correct, it answers all the questions about how a vagina can be neurally so impoverished and yet capable of transmitting sexual sensations.

Women who have uterine and blended orgasms report that they are fully satisfied, wholly satiated, on each occasion of their occurrence.[35] What Sherfey says about the inherent insatiability of the female and her consequent multiorgasmic needs would seem to be applicable only to women who experience nothing but vulval orgasms.[36] From this one may conclude that different kinds of orgasm provide different kinds of satisfaction. It may also be possible to categorize the various types of orgasm in accordance with the distinction between the sensuous and the passionate. There is reason to believe that vulval orgasms are consummations in which the sensuous predominates while uterine orgasms have a special dependency upon the passionate. A *priori*, none of these modes of satisfaction—whether terminative or nonterminative, passionate or sensuous, uterine, vulval or blended—is necessarily preferable to any other.

This chapter has attempted to raise questions for investigation. By clarifying what women *might* mean when they talk about "an orgasm," it is hoped that ultimately sexologists will become aware of the multiplicity of what they *do* mean. A simple, inoffensive question such as, "Do you ever hold your breath during an orgasm?" or "Is your breathing repeatedly interrupted just before the peak?" could help future investigators to identify the type of climax that one or another woman might have. One must recognize, however, that few people are able to analyze their own response at the moment of orgasm. Prior to their respiratory measurements, neither of the Foxes was aware of the repetitive apnea which their experiments showed to be characteristic of Mrs. Fox's preorgasmic breathing pattern.[37] Apparently this is one area of human experience in which even trained physiologists have limited powers of self-observation.

Despite this problem, however, improved questionnaires might reveal many of the orgasmic differences which have thus far been neglected. Most questionnaires now in existence are limited by vagueness in their definition of "orgasm." For example, Wallin and Clark, in their "Study of orgasm as a condition of women's enjoyment in the middle years of marriage," define the word as: "a climax of intense feeling which is followed by a pretty sudden feeling of relief and relaxation."[38] Since this kind of definition applies indiscriminately to all three types of orgasm, many of the results of such studies are cloudy and confusing. New studies are needed to analyze coital enjoyment in the light of the different types of orgasm which we have been discussing.

Equally fascinating would be a statistical analysis of the varieties of foreplay techniques correlated with the types of orgasm. It may well be that the brief, relatively "impoverished" techniques of certain working-class males may be such as to elicit uterine orgasms more frequently than the elaborate foreplay rituals prescribed by current bestsellers on sensuous sexuality. We shall return to this possibility in Chapter 5. Studies of women who experience more than one type of orgasm are needed. And correlations of interpersonal attitudes required for satisfactory lovemaking would also be useful. Malleson quotes one two-type patient who says: "The inside climax comes from loving, but the outside one is just animal feeling."[39] Would other two-type women agree with such a statement, and if so, cannot the word "loving" be analyzed further?

Clearly there is a great need for more physiological data acquired by couples in domestic surroundings with only machines as "observers." The Foxes' experiment on intrauterine pressure needs repeating until data are available from many women for the different types of orgasm. *If* the squeeze-bulb kind of uterine behavior should turn out to be typical for uterine and blended orgasms but not for the vulval orgasm, then Freud's original clitoral-vaginal distinction—freed, if possible, of its normative overtones—might reappear in a physiologically sophisticated form. Freudian analysis of female sexuality needs radical revision; but given the evidence presently available, it seems premature to assert (as Masters and Johnson do) that "clitoral and vaginal orgasms are not separate biologic entities." [40]

By approaching the definition of orgasm in a pluralistic way, as we shall continue to do in later chapters, one can hope to alleviate some of the sexual strictures which recent "how-to" books impose on their public. There is no single correct, definitive, or supremely normal kind of female orgasm. Since people differ in so many aspects of their being, one should expect variability in their modes of sexual satisfaction as well. But obvious as this might seem, psychiatrists and family physicians report that already there are many cases of couples seeking counseling and even divorce because the wife is unable to achieve contractions of the orgasmic platform, even though she responds with great emotional enjoyment to coitus. Many of the young are also confused. The psychiatrist Judianne Densen-Gerber has recently remarked: "The teen-age girl hung up on the idea of female orgasm ends up by humiliating her masculinity-obsessed but usually inexperienced partner. This syndrome is the major route to youthful drug addiction." [41]

Perhaps the most misunderstood women of all are those who enjoy coitus without an orgasm of any kind. Helene Deutsch believes that these women are the most "typical" and the most "feminine." [42] Malleson also defends these women:

> For a great many married couples, this doctrine of the overvaluation of orgasm is disturbing, since it puts a false emphasis on one limited factor in the whole sexual relationship. Such teaching tacitly implies that the mere presence or absence of orgasm should be the criterion of successful intimacy. Apart from the fact that orgasm is by no means possible for many women, people cannot measure their deepest feeling by a physical response. No one would dream of saying that a person could not really be happy unless he were heard to laugh, nor feel sorrow unless his tears could be seen. [43]

It seems reasonable to believe that there are many different patterns of healthy sexual adjustment, some orgasmic and others not. One must also recognize that the analysis I have given may not encompass all varieties of what women might justifiably call an orgasm. Too little is known about human sexual response for any analysis to claim that it is comprehensive.

Chapter 4

———————— ◆◆◆ ————————

THE
CLITORAL-VAGINAL
TRANSFER THEORY

Freud is usually credited with the original formulation of the clitoral-vaginal transfer theory. What he says on the subject is, however, rather meager compared to the importance which so many of his followers have given to this theory. It is in fact astonishing that Freud himself should have said so little about something that he considered "intimately related to the essence of femininity," and one of "the chief determinants of the greater proneness of women to neurosis." [1] The initial formulation occurs in the *Three Essays on the Theory of Sexuality*, first published in 1905. Freud there says the following:

> If the woman finally submits to the sexual act, the clitoris becomes stimulated and its role is to conduct the excitement to the adjacent genital parts; it acts here like a chip of pinewood, which is utilized to set fire to the harder wood. It often takes some time before this transference is accomplished, and during this transition the young wife remains anesthetic. This anesthesia

may become permanent if the clitoric zone refuses to give up its excitability; a condition brought on by profuse sexual activities in infantile life. It is known that anesthesia in women is often only apparent and local. They are anesthetic at the vaginal entrance, but not at all unexcitable through the clitoris or even through other zones. . . .

If the transference of the erogenous excitability from the clitoris to the vaginal entrance succeeds, the woman then changes her leading zone for the future sexual activity; the man, on the other hand, retains his from childhood.[2]

This statement includes vagaries which we will have to examine further. The mere wording of the first clause is problematic, and nowhere does the text explain why the clitoris should have to give up its excitability if it is so useful as kindling. At the outset, however, this passage may be sufficient to indicate the broad outlines of Freud's general theory. Prior to puberty, he believes, girls have little awareness of their vagina; after puberty they begin to transfer their erotic sensitivity from the clitoris to the vagina; and unless this occurs, they cannot become mature or authentically feminine women. In the lines I have just quoted, Freud stresses the importance of the clitoris *losing* its sensitivity once the vagina becomes excitable. This idea was reiterated in 1917:

In her childhood, moreover, a girl's clitoris takes on the role of a penis entirely: it is characterized by special excitability and is the area in which autoerotic satisfaction is obtained. The process of a girl's becoming a woman depends very much on the clitoris passing on this sensitivity to the vaginal orifice in good time and completely. In cases of what is known as sexual anaesthesia in women the clitoris has obstinately retained its sensitivity.[3]

It would seem therefore that Freud expects female children to start out with one type of sexuality and then to progress into another, with still a third as an intermediary stage (the stage in which the clitoris acts as kindling). But in 1933 he implied that the intermediate stage was just as normal a goal for mature women as any other:

. . . in the phallic phase of girls the clitoris is the leading erotogenic zone. But it is not, of course, going to remain so. With the change to femininity the clitoris should wholly *or in part* hand over its sensitivity, and at the same time its importance, to the vagina.[4]

I have italicized "or in part" because this formulation of the clitoral-vaginal transfer theory would seem to allow the clitoris an ultimate importance which the original formulation clearly denied to it.

Freud's development as a thinker is often characterized by a long series of revisions and reapproximations. In this case, however, he gives us little from which to determine whether his later language is meant as a refinement upon the earlier. Specifically, we do not know whether Freud considered clitoral sensitivity to be necessarily a deterrent to the attainment of sexual maturity. It is clear, however, that he thought that the clitoris must become at least secondary in importance.

Since Freud himself never distinguishes between clitoral and vaginal *orgasm*, that distinction having developed among his followers, and since his language is ambiguous, it will be more fruitful to analyze the clitoral-vaginal transfer theory as it occurs in the more sophisticated versions it was later to receive. Here, however, one should point out that it is hard to know what Freud means by "the *leading* erotogenic zone," or what exactly was involved in the giving up of "clitoral excitability." Did he mean that a mature woman would become anesthetic at the clitoris? Or did he mean that she would feel a yearning for coitus which may have begun with clitoral sensitivity but which eventuates in vaginal excitation? Was he advocating one area of local stimulation as preferable to another? Was he referring to different kinds of foreplay? And was he talking about physiological processes, postulating that the development of the normal female involves a change from one biological system to another?

I think these questions are unanswerable in terms of what Freud himself actually wrote. Leaving aside doubts that some Freudians have expressed about vaginal anesthesia in the young girl, the following theses seem to be the principal ones that were finally generated out of Freud's brief statements:

(1) There are at least two types of orgasmic experience which women may undergo. Alexander Lowen describes the difference between clitoral and vaginal orgasms as follows:

. . . the vaginal orgasm is experienced in the depths of the body, the clitoral reaction is limited to the surface. From what [women patients] say, it appears that only the vaginal orgasm produces the feelings of fulfillment, complete release and satisfaction. In my years of clinical experience as a psychiatrist, I never heard a woman assert anything to the contrary.[5]

Lowen also presents the following reports from two of his patients:

The clitoral orgasm is felt on the surface of the vagina like a trickle of sweet pleasure. There is no satisfying release. The vaginal orgasm is like the opening of a dam which floods my body with pleasure and leaves me with a feeling of deep release and satisfaction. There is no comparison. The next day after a clitoral orgasm, I am hot, disturbed. After the other, I wake up in one piece, relaxed.

The vaginal orgasm I experience, limited as it may be, fills me with a sense of completeness, of satisfaction. I have a feeling of being full—filled up. The clitoral orgasm is more high level in excitement but leaves me with no aftereffect of completion. I feel I could have one clitoral orgasm right after another.[6]

Writing in 1970, Robert Robertiello formulates the distinction in a similar fashion:

As a psychoanalyst who has discussed sexual responses for many years with many women who have absolutely no reason to distort the truth, I do not doubt that there are two distinct kinds of sexual responses in women. There are two easily distinguishable kinds of orgasms as they are subjectively experienced. The clitoral orgasm, which is so called because in most women it can be elicited by manually stroking the clitoris, is a very intense, rather short-lasting response which builds to a rapid crescendo and falls just as rapidly. It is closer to the usual sexual response of the male. The so-called vaginal response is one that is more frequently reached during intercourse and rises more slowly, does not reach such a sharp peak, lasts much longer, falls off much more slowly and usually gives a deeper and fuller feeling of satisfaction. To women who have both kinds of orgasm, the distinction is very clear. The vaginal one is usually preferred although there is considerable satisfaction in the clitoral orgasm as well.

Many women experience no orgasm at all. Many more women experience only clitoral orgasms. A smaller percentage of women experience both kinds of orgasm.[7]

Two years after Freud's later statement, the psychoanalyst Sylvia Payne suggested a distinction between three types of orgasm, which she refers to as the clitoral, the vaginal, and the "merged":

> I shall take first the feminine orgasm. A study of the physical side reveals the fact that orgasm of the vagina which may include muscular contraction of the uterus can be distinguished from orgasm associated with clitoral erotism. One may and I think should be merged into the other, but they are frequently easily distinguishable. Vaginal orgasm has a sucking characteristic, and in some cases the uterus may definitely retract up slightly into the pelvis. Clitoral orgasm is a discharging orgasm and is more like the male orgasm.[8]

(2) A woman is to be considered "frigid" (i.e., sexually and even emotionally deficient) if she is unable to have sexual experiences that eventuate in vaginal orgasm. Karl Abraham maintains that "in frigidity . . . the pleasurable sensation is as a rule situated in the clitoris and the vaginal zone has none." [9] Bergler and Kroger explicitly state:

> Frigidity is the incapacity of a woman to achieve a vaginal orgasm during intercourse. It is of no matter whether the woman is aroused during coitus or remains cold, whether excitement is weak or strong, whether it breaks off at the beginning or ends slowly or suddenly, whether it is dissipated in preliminary acts, or has been lacking from the beginning. The only criterion of frigidity is absence of vaginal orgasm.[10]

Not all psychoanalysts who accept Freud's distinction between the clitoral and the vaginal modes of experience go as far as Bergler and Kroger in this concept of frigidity; but something of the sort would seem to be implied by Freud's insistence upon the vagina as the dominant erotic zone in what he considers to be normal and mature women.

(3) Sensitivity in and stimulation of the clitoris tends to make it impossible for a woman to experience the feelings that accompany the vaginal orgasm in coitus. Lowen says:

> I do not mean to condemn the practice of clitoral stimulation if a woman finds that this is the way that she can obtain a sexual release. Above all, she should not feel guilty about using this procedure. However, I advise my patients against this practice since it focuses feeling on the clitoris and prevents the vaginal response.[11]

And Marie Robinson tells us that women who have difficulty achieving the vaginal orgasm should be encouraged to abandon clitoral gratification: "We have found that, if the clitoridal woman wishes to achieve a more mature form of sexual satisfaction, she may be aided in reaching her goal if she can give up the form of gratification she now employs." [12] This kind of recommendation conforms to Freud's idea that normal vaginal sensitivity requires a diminution in the importance given to the clitoris. But since Freud, as in the 1933 statement, leaves open the possibility that the clitoris may retain at least some of its earlier excitability, it is conceivable that he himself would have agreed with psychoanalysts such as Rado. With the Lowen–Robinson type of attitude in mind, Rado insists:

> In the healthy female, clitoral and vaginal stimulation complement each other in the production of sexual arousal and orgasmic satisfaction. By suppressing her clitoral sensations, the female cannot possibly augment her vaginal responses; she can only reduce her capacity for sexual performance, health and happiness.[13]

(4) Implicit in the statements of Freud's followers, as well as Freud himself, is the belief that masturbation—which in women is generally a function of clitoral sensitivity—is inherently immature. When Freud speaks of the necessity for a transfer from the clitoral to the vaginal as the principal erotic zone, he partly means to suggest that an interest in masturbation does not characterize the sexuality of a truly mature woman. And though some of his followers tolerate masturbation as a subsidiary activity on the part of the healthy-minded woman, they more or less agree with this dictum.

In some ways the most interesting (and the most maligned and misunderstood) of the Freudian theorists in the area of female sexuality is Marie Bonaparte. She was a sexologist in a sense in which Freud himself was not. Even in writings like the *Three Essays on the Theory of Sexuality*, Freud rarely discusses the sex act itself, and he scarcely suggests what he thinks it might be like for women. Bonaparte makes up this deficiency at the same time as her analyses remain faithful to the Freudian inspiration from which they derive their theoretical framework. Bonaparte takes most of her ideas from Freud, but also her unswerving belief in the clitoral-vaginal transfer theory must have served to confirm the doctrine in Freud's mind.

Marie Bonaparte was a younger woman to whom Freud turned for counsel in trying to fathom the enigmas of female sexuality. It was to her that he addressed his oft-quoted query about the inscrutable female:

> The great question that has never been answered and which I have not yet been able to answer, despite my thirty years of research into the feminine soul, is "What does a woman want?" [14]

In itself, this question (*"Was will das Weib?"*) is indicative of Freud's limitations as a thinker. Why should he assume that there is one thing which all women want simply *by virtue of* their being women? Would he ever have asked himself or any male colleague "What does a *man* want?" Different men want different things on different occasions. Freud recognized this. Apparently he could not see that the same was true of women.

I wonder what Bonaparte could have replied. One assumes that, though she was still in her twenties at the time she was asked, her personal experience must have reinforced Freud's belief in the clitoral-vaginal transfer theory. Freud's dates are 1856–1939. Bonaparte's are 1882–1962. In order to be able to look back on "thirty years of research," Freud must have been about fifty or fifty-five when he made the remark. This would date the conversation to a time soon after the 1905 publication of the *Three Essays*. Bonaparte would have been in her middle or late twenties. By the time that her book *Female Sexuality* appeared more than four decades later, her thinking had progressed to a point where the clitoral-vaginal transfer theory had become part of an elaborate typology. The book is itself an attempt to answer Freud's fundamental question, and it does so by spelling out the implications of the transfer theory in terms of Bonaparte's five-fold analysis.

Bonaparte's classification of heterosexual women is worth considering in itself, but it takes on particular interest if one compares it with what we have already said about the three types of female orgasm. Where Freud talks always in terms of clitoral *vs.* vaginal "sensitivity" or "excitability," Bonaparte addresses herself to the possibility of there being a diversity among the orgasms which different kinds of women actually experience. The word "orgasm" she does not formally define, but for her it seems to mean "the violent discharge of an explosive accumulation of libido." [15] This seems rather uninteresting as either a definition or a characterization, but clearly what interests Bonaparte most is her analysis of the different types.

The heroines of Bonaparte's typology are the women she calls "vaginal" or "solely vaginal." These are orgasmic women for whom sex is "all but reduced to simple coitus." [16] Insisting that they "have achieved maximum adaptation to the erotic function," Bonaparte says that "such women remain insensitive to, or are irritated by, clitoridal caresses. . . . Only coitus will release orgastic pleasure and orgasm in these." [17] Perhaps it is significant that Bonaparte talks of "orgastic pleasure *and* orgasm" in these women. She seems to imply that there must be women who are not sure whether to call their reaction an "orgasm" or not. There may be women, for example, who would say that they have orgastic *pleasure*, even though they would not know whether they have had an orgasm. There may be women who find the sexual experience so overwhelming that they can scarcely classify it with any accuracy. Bonaparte obviously includes such women in her "vaginal" category provided they meet its other criteria.

It seems plausible to assume that Bonaparte's "vaginal" females are women who have a facility for uterine orgasms. They would even seem to be women who have no orgasms other than uterine orgasms. Speaking of them, Bonaparte says, "In coitus, the woman, in effect, is subjected to a sort of beating by the man's penis. She receives its blows and often, even, loves their violence." [18] Such "violence" would seem to indicate the kind of strong, accelerating, deep, and relatively brief thrusting that is best suited to the uterine orgasm. Bonaparte talks of the necessity of a "deep and truly vaginal sensitivity to the blows of the penis." [19] This sensitivity may very well be related to the pleasurable peritoneal stimulation which uterine jostling induces. Bonaparte stresses the importance of female "passivity" throughout her book. Though she may mean other things as well, she appears to be advocating a type of coital behavior in which the woman keeps her pelvis immobile while lying flat on her back. Such a woman would indeed be more passive than a woman who aims for a blended or vulval orgasm and therefore moves her pelvis in order to enhance vulval (and clitoral) friction. Bonaparte implies that the "normal" position is preferred by the type of woman she calls vaginal whereas her so-called clitoridal women find it an impediment. Vulval contraction she mentions only once in the whole book: "As to orgasms of a vaginal origin, it is even less possible to vouch for them from the purely 'behaviorist' viewpoint, for any contractions that accompany it may also have been present before." [20] In other words, if a woman is accustomed to having nonterminative vulval orgasms en route to her blended orgasms, Bonaparte denies the significance of the vulval contractions in the final blended orgasm. Although the blended orgasm may, as a matter of fact, be quite different from the sum of its parts, all that Bonaparte really cares about is the uterine component.

This brings us to Bonaparte's thumbnail sketch of women who have blended orgasms:

> Next come those women with vaginal and clitoridal erotogenicity harmoniously attuned. Such women are capable of orgastic pleasure through clitoridal caresses, but generally prefer to keep them as a preliminary to coitus: a necessary preparative if some functional retardation be present. In any case, with such women, in coitus, both vagina *and* clitoris play their part in concert. . . . [21] [Her italics.]

To a contemporary reader, such a woman might seem to be the ideal female; and one must wonder why Bonaparte is convinced that only her first type of woman, the solely vaginal, has achieved "maximum adaptation to the erotic function."

In contrast to women who have blended orgasms, Bonaparte describes others who vacillate back and forth between the vulval and uterine responses. These "either/or" females, as I shall call them, Bonaparte characterizes as follows:

> Other women again, while possessing this composite function, may also achieve the orgasm through each of these *separate* zones: via the vagina *or* the clitoris. These are often women who feel the vagina and the clitoris to be mutually antagonistic: now one, now the other, plays its part. In such women, orgastic sensation in coitus is generally only vaginal.[22] [Her italics.]

In fluctuating between the uterine and the vulval types of orgasm, either/or women do not blend the two in any single experience. Their normal pattern consists in the alternation between Bonaparte's "vaginal" and "clitoridal" types of sexuality. Of the latter she says:

> Another category of women consists of those clitoridals with whom we have already dealt at length. In such women, the viriloid phallic function predominates at the expense of a more, or less, undeveloped or inhibited vaginalism.[23]

Ignoring Bonaparte's pejorative terminology, one may say that these women are defined by their capacity for having nothing but vulval orgasms. In calling them "clitoridals" and in remarking that the preliminaries of sensuous foreplay serve as the "sole sustenance" of so many clitoridals, Bonaparte's category also includes women who derive their vulval orgasms through noncoital behavior.[24] This makes sense in view of the fact that the vulval orgasm resulting from masturbation or other extravaginal stimulation is substantially the same as the vulval orgasm resulting from coitus. The either/or woman, whose orgastic sensation during coitus is "generally only vaginal," would seem to experience uterine orgasms in coitus and vulval orgasms through extracoital means.

Finally, Bonaparte describes a kind of woman she calls "wholly frigid." Unlike those Freudians who use this term for all females who do not experience "vaginal" orgasms, Bonaparte employs it only for women who derive no pleasure from heterosexual behavior of any sort:

> . . . there are . . . women in whom a total inhibition of both erotogenic zones has occurred. These are the wholly frigid. Neither coitus, nor the most varied caresses of the male, will avail to give them pleasure.[25]

Still other kinds of women should be added to this list: those who derive pleasure from sexual experiences without being orgasmic, those who sometimes have vulval orgasms and sometimes have blended orgasms, and those who experience all three types on one or another occasion. In the majority of published statements in which one woman describes two types of orgasm, it is impossible to determine whether she is referring to blended-and-vulval orgasms or uterine-and-vulval orgasms. Hilda O'Hare, for instance, is cited by both Ellis and D. G. Brown as an example of a two-type woman; but a careful reading of her texts leaves the crucial question unanswered: in her "vaginal orgasms" did she or did she not have vulval contractions?[26] I have encountered one woman whose description of her experience would indicate that she must be a three-type female. As yet, there are no comparable case histories in the literature.

Criticism of the Freudian and post-Freudian distinction between clitoral and vaginal responses began to accumulate in the late 1940s; but it is Kinsey's report on the female in 1953 that first mounts a detailed and systematic attack. Although Kinsey states that many women, "and perhaps a majority of them," distinguish between a type of satisfaction that results from coitus involving deep vaginal penetration and one that results from stimulation of the labia or clitoris alone, he considers the vaginal orgasm to be a "biologic impossibility."[27] As against the Freudian suppositions that existed at the time he was writing, his arguments are quite impressive. Nevertheless they are inadequate for the conclusions he wishes to draw. After each of his points I shall try to provide a rejoinder based upon the analysis of types of female orgasm which has already been outlined.

(1) The vagina, Kinsey tells us, is devoid of end organs of touch. "In most females the walls of the vagina . . . are quite insensitive when they are gently stroked or lightly pressed." [28] Though undoubtedly true, this is uninteresting as far as vigorous thrusting in coitus is concerned. The uterine and blended orgasms depend upon a jostling of the cervix which can hardly happen without deep vaginal penetration, but the pleasure that results from such jostling need not involve any special sensitivity in the walls of the vagina. If the evidence about the peritoneum as a locus of orgasmic sensation is creditable, then the fact of vaginal insensitivity is simply irrelevant.

(2) To emphasize the insignificance of the vagina as a sexual locus, Kinsey remarks that it can even be cut painlessly. As early as 1949, Malleson had already criticized him on this point:

I would disagree entirely with his assumption that because the vagina is anatomically "less supplied by nerves" than the clitoris that its qualitative and quantitative sensation must therefore be less. One can cut the intestine of a sentient patient without hurting him; but stretch it and you have agony. You can cut or cauterize the cervix with little pain, but stretch it No: or give it friction under emotional circumstances and quite another type of sensation will be engendered.[29]

(3) Kinsey points out that relatively few females masturbate by making deep vaginal insertions. But this is easily accounted for by the fact that masturbation is generally used as a means of effecting vulval orgasms, and for that purpose a woman need only resort to clitoral manipulation. One occasionally encounters women who claim to have had "vaginal orgasms" as a result of masturbation, but it is difficult to know what it is that they are reporting. Possibly an earlier experience of blended or uterine orgasm is being duplicated in the imagination during the process of clitoral masturbation. It would be surprising if the physiology of uterine and blended orgasms occurred under these circumstances, but it is not inconceivable that some reflex action on the

part of the uterus might operate as a result of the sexual fantasy itself. In any event, though the usual pattern of masturbation does not ordinarily involve vaginal insertions, this cannot militate against the fact that when such insertions are made in the course of natural coitus there sometimes ensues a kind of orgasm quite different from the kind which requires no insertions whatsoever.

(4) As further corroboration, Kinsey remarks that in homosexual relations between females one rarely encounters attempts at deep vaginal insertion. From this too, however, one can only infer that female homosexuality may provide vulval orgasms without affording the kinds that depend upon heterosexual intercourse of a coital sort. It may merely be a lack of technological facility which prevents the dildo from duplicating the effect of a man's penis, but possibly there are also psychological and emotional reasons for the failure to provide uterine and blended orgasms. This is an area in which one has hardly any evidence. Accustomed as they are to vulval orgasms, homosexual partners have probably little awareness of the pleasures to be derived from deep coital penetration. It is quite conceivable that females *could* manage to provide each other with orgasms related to the enjoyable stimulation of the cervix and the peritoneum. But as yet one has no reason to think that this often happens.

(5) As against Freud's notion that a transfer from clitoral to vaginal interests occurs in the course of a woman's normal development, Kinsey denies that there are sexual phases of that sort through which females progress:

> The individual difference in patterns of response are quite persistent throughout an individual's lifetime, and probably depend upon inherent capacities more than upon learned acquirements. . . . No question of "maturity" seems to be involved. . . .[30]

Kinsey may very well be right in thinking that by and large women do not change in their patterns of response, and therefore that the clitoral-vaginal theory must be wrong in postulating a characteristic transfer. But even if Kinsey is right in this, his generalization does not undermine the distinction between types of orgasm. And if one were to formulate questionnaires on the basis of that distinction, one might find instances of development that

Kinsey was simply unable to detect with his conceptual equipment. An interviewer who neglects to ask a woman about the different kinds of orgasm which she has had on different occasions may overestimate the pervasiveness of one or another response. If, however, one recognizes that even vulval contractions can occur within diverse orgasmic patterns, one may discover variations throughout a period of time which could reopen the possibility of a transfer of sensitivity. Some women do report that their orgasms, and even their ideas of what it is to have an orgasm, change in the course of a lifetime.

Kinsey is particularly concerned to deny the possibility of a clitoral-vaginal transfer because he thinks that therapists who try to encourage it in their patients are wasting their time and possibly causing psychological damage. But here again one can argue that even if the transfer cannot be established as a genetic development in most or all women who receive the honorific label of "maturity," nevertheless the distinction between types of orgasm may provide one among many tools that therapists can use in helping a woman to find a means of sexual expression which is authentically her own.

Kinsey lists several possible sources of the satisfactions which are obtainable from deep vaginal penetration. He believes that some or all of these may be involved on any particular occasion. What he says is highly suggestive, and wholly compatible with the distinction between the different types of orgasm for which I have been arguing:

(1) Psychologic satisfaction in knowing that a sexual union and deep penetration have been effected. The realization that the partner is being satisfied may be a factor of considerable importance here.

(2) Tactile stimulation coming from the full body contact with the partner, and from his weight. This may result in pressures on various internal organs which can produce "referred sensations." These may be incorrectly interpreted as coming from surface stimulation.

(3) Tactile stimulation by the male genitalia or body pressing against the labia minora, the clitoris, or the vestibule of the

vagina. This alone would provide sufficient stimulation to bring most females to orgasm. The location of this stimulation may be correctly recognized or it may be incorrectly attributed to the interior of the vagina.

(4) Stimulation of the levator ring of muscles in coitus. Such stimulation may bring reflex spasms which may have distinctly erotic significance.

(5) Stimulation of the nerves that lie on the perineal muscle mass (the so-called pelvic sling), which is located between the rectum and the vagina.

(6) The direct stimulation, in some females, of end organs in the walls of the vagina itself. But this can be true only of the 14 percent who are conscious of tactile stimulation of the area. There is, however, no evidence that the vagina is ever the sole source of arousal, or even the primary source of erotic arousal in any female.[31]

In making his enumeration, Kinsey missed the single most relevant source of satisfaction, namely the pleasure resulting from peritoneal stimulation when the woman's viscera are jostled by the penis. By 1949, LeMon Clark had already mentioned this as an effect that cannot be accounted for by those who think that all orgasms are alike.[32] Kinsey misses this point entirely; but in talking about the experience of deep penetration, he does give himself a clue:

> There is a parallel situation in anal coitus. The anus, like the entrance to the vagina, is richly supplied with nerves, but the rectum, like the depths of the vagina, is a tube which is poorly supplied with sensory nerves. However, the receiving partner, female or male, often reports that the deep penetration of the rectum may bring satisfaction which is, in many respects, comparable to that which may be obtained from a deep vaginal insertion.[33]

Kinsey seems puzzled by this evidence, and he never analyzes the implications of there being a comparable satisfaction in the two kinds of sexual experience. But at least he struggles with the problem of deep penetration as something women find satisfying.

As early as 1962, Masters and Johnson concluded that there
was no evidence to support the clitoral-vaginal transfer theory. In
their experimental studies they could find nothing to distinguish
one kind of female orgasm from another. In an article they published that year, they say that orgasms do not differ among themselves regardless of how they are elicited—"whether as a result of
clitoral area manipulation, natural or artificial coition, or, for that
matter, breast manipulation alone." [34] At least with respect to
the biological criteria, they could detect nothing that would support the Freudian theory: "The human female's physiologic responses to effective sexual stimulation develop with consistency
regardless of the source of the psychic or physical stimulation." [35]
In the book *Human Sexual Response*, the language seems more
sweeping:

> From an anatomic point of view, there is absolutely no difference
> in the responses of the pelvic viscera to effective sexual stimula-
> tion, regardless of whether the stimulation occurs as a result of
> clitoral-body or mons area manipulation, natural or artificial
> coition, or, for that matter, specific stimulation of any other
> erogenous area of the female body.[36]

We seem to have come a long way from Kinsey, who certainly
did not believe that there was "absolutely no difference" in responses of the pelvic viscera. For one thing, Kinsey was testifying
as a sociologist who gathered data from whatever women he was
able to interview. At least, these women were not chosen in advance on the basis of their sexual performance. It is significant
that he makes no reference to "effective" sexual stimulation, since
that concept involves a standard of achievement which he refused
to impose upon his population sample. Unlike Masters and Johnson, he was not an experimentalist; he did not have to decide
which women he would observe. Masters and Johnson had to
make decisions of this sort, and—as I have been suggesting—they
made them in a way that distorts or even falsifies the actual differences between different orgasmic responses. Simply on the face of
it, what they say in the passage just quoted cannot be the truth.
A woman's pelvic viscera *must* respond differently if they are
being subjected to a "beating" (to use Bonaparte's word) rather

than the mild stimulation which results from a gentle massage of the clitoris. In the first case, the viscera are being forced to move by contact with the thrusting penis. In the second case, the reactions are more indirect, particularly since they do not depend upon peritoneal stimulation. Furthermore, it is worth mentioning that R. P. Michael has recently shown that natural and artificial coition induce different patterns of uterine response in rhesus monkeys. In natural coition, the uterus contracts repeatedly with the precise rhythm of the thrusting penis. When an artificial phallus was substituted, the uterine behavior produced "a quite different type of record." [37]

In their second book, *Human Sexual Inadequacy*, Masters and Johnson reveal the therapeutic consequences of defining orgasm as they do. Women who complain of orgasmic incapacity are taught how to attain the vulval orgasm. The criterion of success in sexual adjustment becomes the rhythmic contractions of the orgasmic platform. Husbands are discouraged from any kind of behavior which makes it less likely that the wife will achieve this goal. At least in their training period, the couple must avoid the kind of passionate thrusting which may be essential for uterine and blended orgasms. As opposed to "goal-oriented demand," the wife is told to "allow the vaginally contained penis to stimulate slowly and feelingly in the same manner she enjoyed sensate pleasure from manual body stroking or the manipulation of her genital organs under her controlled directions." [38] For women who find uterine orgasms easy to attain but have difficulty achieving vulval or blended orgasms, such advice may be quite beneficial. Similarly, a woman who has no orgasms because she has never learned to enjoy sensate pleasures of any kind can certainly profit from a therapeutic program that systematically encourages her to relax and have a good time sexually. But as a general recommendation, such advice suffers from the same limitations as the underlying theory on which it is based.

Though a sexologist cannot define any types of orgasm out of existence, he can—if he is sufficiently influential—change sexual behavior in such a way as to minimize their occurrence. It is for this reason that the concepts of Masters and Johnson are potentially harmful. A woman who has a vulval orgasm may sometimes

find the event singularly unrewarding. She may require something
else, or something more, out of sexual experience and she is done
a considerable disservice if she is simply told that all orgasms are
alike and so there *is* nothing else to be expected. At least nothing
physical or anatomical, with the implication that women delude
themselves if they claim to undergo more than the twitching of
the orgasmic platform which, along with some other physiological
concomitants, nature has appointed as the instrumentality of
female sexual response. For all its scientific crudity, the Freudian
doctrine did at least recognize that orgasm at the superfices of
the genital tract need not be fully satisfying. Freud and his followers erred in thinking that women for whom it was sufficient must
be abnormal or pathological. Masters and Johnson err in thinking
that other women, those who find libidinal release in blended and
uterine orgasms, must be responding to "subjective" influences
for which there is no biologic correlate.

The problem that Freud nowadays presents to sexology is aptly
epitomized by an anonymous critic, scribbling in the fly-leaf of a
college library copy of Bonaparte's *Female Sexuality*:

This book is mostly terrifying bullshit.

Masters and Johnson have proved conclusively that there is no
difference in a "vaginal" and clitoral orgasm. The clitoris is the
center of all female sexuality (labia minora are also sensitive).
Pleasure through coitus is either directly or indirectly clitoral.
The vagina is tough, elastic, insensitive.

Freud was just indulging his own fucked-up male chauvinist
fantasies.

Pleasure to the People!

As against such polemical ardor, one can only cite the evidence
of a gynecologist such as LeMon Clark, whose conclusions I have
already mentioned several times. His most recent discussion of
these problems, in a 1970 article entitled, "Is there a difference
between a clitoral and a vaginal orgasm?," is worth quoting at
length:

Some women objected to the use of the vaginal diaphragm stating that it took away a great deal of feeling. It occurred to me that this might result from the rubber dome of the diaphragm deflecting the penis so that it did not move the cervix as much as it did without the diaphragm. Moving the cervix would move the uterus and the broad ligament, both of which are covered with peritoneum, one of the most sensitive organs in the body. This would give a much broader base for sensation in the whole lower abdominal area than mere stimulation of the clitoris alone.

At that time I had available a laboratory for the manufacture of diaphragms. I made some with a dome as thin as the rubber in a condom, so that it would not deflect the penis. This solved the problem for these women. They enjoyed normal sensation with a diaphragm.

During my intern days, thirty-three years ago, I was brought up with the thought of the time that a sub-total hysterectomy was the operation of choice because a total hysterectomy meant opening the vagina, and the danger of infection and peritonitis was too great. Thirty years ago I went to Vienna and learned how to do a vaginal hysterectomy. I never shall forget the shock I received after doing a vaginal hysterectomy upon a patient and getting what was, operatively speaking, a perfect result. Two or three months later she came in and wanted to know what was the matter with her, she no longer enjoyed intercourse because she "felt just dead up inside." She was, of course, no longer getting any stimulation of the cervix, uterus, and broad ligaments as she had before the operation. I have had several women voice the same complaint following a total hysterectomy.

For quite another reason failure to achieve cervical, uterine stimulation robbed a woman of her capacity to achieve orgasm and left her very upset emotionally. She had been married for 17 years to her first husband, who had died. His penis was something over eight inches long and two inches in diameter. After his death she married again, a man she loved and who was very good and kind to her, but, she said, "I would judge by sight that his penis is only between four and five inches long at most and much smaller in diameter." She simply could not reach orgasm with him and was left frustrated and had become nervous and depressed, since she desperately did not want to hurt her husband's feelings by admitting this to him.

Recently another test occurred to me which rather clearly

demonstrates the contribution which vaginal stimulation makes in giving satisfaction to the woman. Someone gave me an electric tooth brush which we never used. It cluttered up the bathroom and my wife wanted it out of the way. I was just about to throw it out when it occurred to me that there was another type of vibrator.

I had a rubber vaginal dilator about seven inches long and an inch in diameter. The rubber was flexible, smooth, elastic but firm. By punching a hole in its base with a sharp knife I could put it on the vibrating tip of the tooth brush. It had a relatively slow (compared to an ordinary electric vibrator) but definite vibration.

Shortly after this I had a patient who had never reached orgasm. The electric vibrator even failed to induce one. As she was an intelligent individual I suggested that I try the vaginal vibrator in conjunction with the ordinary clitoral stimulation. Within three or four minutes she reached a rather intense orgasm. I have had three cases in which the two vibrators have been combined. I have tried the ordinary clitoral vibrator first and then the two combined and have asked the patient to estimate the amount of increased sensation. One said it was 40 percent greater, one said 60 percent greater, and one said, rather enthusiastically, that it was 75 percent greater, and was a much more pleasurable sensation than she had ever had from intercourse.[39]

More recently, Clark has had similar evidence from a considerably larger number of subjects.[40] The peritoneum, which he identifies as the sensitive organ in so-called vaginal orgasms, provides feelings which also result from an interesting gamut of nonsexual experiences. Not only is the peritoneum stimulated by deep thrusting of the penis, as in uterine and blended orgasms, but also by the dislocation of the viscera when an elevator suddenly rises, or in the course of a steep roller-coaster ride, or while bounding over a hillock in the back seat of an automobile. These sensations are sometimes recognized by women as being quasi-sexual. They gasp on such occasions, as if in the onset of apnea, and in other ways as well seem to approximate miniature orgasmic experience. Men too have a peritoneum, which may be stimulated through homosexual anal intercourse. This may account for the fact that men in such relations sometimes speak of having experienced a "vaginal orgasm" comparable to what women describe. Certainly there is reason to think that in the elevator and roller-coaster situations men feel comparable sensations. From this, one may conclude that though the uterus provides an anatomical factor that cannot be present in the male, it is the contact with the peritoneum which accounts for the orgasmic character of deep penetration in either the uterine or the blended orgasm. On the other hand, men rarely identify the stimulation of the peritoneum in extrasexual situations as being quasi-erotic. Perhaps this is due to the fact that, in heterosexual intercourse at least, the male's peritoneum is not involved in any systematic way. But possibly it also indicates a difference in sensation that results from the having of a uterus. One needs further evidence from women who have undergone hysterectomies and from homosexuals who engage in anal intercourse.

Until more research is done to determine the significance of the peritoneum in both men and women, as well as the relevance of other physiological correlates in the different types of orgasm, one can only make tentative hypotheses about Freud's basic dichotomy. It seems reasonable to believe, however, that a woman never "gives up" any erotic sensitivity once it has been acquired. Freud spoke of a *transfer*, but surely these earlier capacities are less likely to disappear with maturation than to pervade and subtly influence later stages of development. There is much reason to believe that girls who masturbate at an early age, bringing themselves to orgasm with facility through mere clitoral stimulation, are likely to have no difficulty in experiencing vulval orgasm through coitus once their post-pubertal sexual interests have developed. For the blended orgasm, more than this facility alone is needed; but what distinguishes the blended from the uterine orgasm is partly the occurrence of vulval contractions, and that would seem to be a function of a clitoral eroticism which has not completely disappeared with the attainment of maturity. The clitoral-vaginal transfer theory entails a radical shift in feminine sexuality from "clitoridal" girls, in Bonaparte's analysis, to "vaginal" women. There seems to be little or no evidence to support the idea that any such transformation normally occurs, even in those preferential types that the Freudians would consider "mature." [41]

The argument of Masters and Johnson depends upon their belief that the clitoris is always stimulated—directly or indirectly—in normal coitus, and that it functions in a similar way in all orgasms. As I have already suggested, the first part of this statement one can readily accept, but the second needs further investigation and is probably false. An either/or woman tends to feel that the clitoris is the erotic center for her vulval orgasms but not for her uterine orgasms. Other women find the clitoris rather unimportant for their orgasmic experience as a whole. The clitoris sometimes feels no more involved than the inner thighs, the abdomen, or other sensitive parts of the body. Is it *likely* that clitoris physiology remains the same throughout these different kinds of orgasms as experienced by different types of women? It would be surprising if this were so.

Throughout these conceptual difficulties, and in the face of the inadequate evidence which the primitive science of sexology has thus far provided, Malleson remains as the most rational and the most unbiased of all authorities in the field. Without pretending that all women are alike, or even that we know as yet just how they differ among themselves, she prepares us for finding that here, as elsewhere, women belong to a highly diversified population:

> It is not easy to say what proportion of women have more feeling in the outer clitoral area than in the vagina itself. Possibly about a third of civilized women get their climax externally; perhaps another third achieve it mainly in the vaginal passage, and another third achieve it seldom or never. Of women who can reach it from either area it is found that the inner climax is generally—but not quite always—the one most valued. It is held by psychiatrists that the emotional content of the two types of orgasm is different. Most women will confirm this, though there can be no question of the significance being identical for everybody. Thus one woman stated: "I *love* with the internal one, the outer is just sheer pleasure." Another woman who greatly enjoyed clitoral orgasm felt "shocked and ill" after a vaginal one.[42] [Italics in text.]

Chapter 5

————————— ◆ ◆ —————————

TWO SYSTEMS
OF SEXUAL MORES

In his book on the male, Kinsey repeatedly contrasts two distinct "systems of mores," two behavioral patterns for sexual intercourse. One of them "depends on prolonged pre-coital play, a considerable variety in techniques, a maximum of stimulation before coital union, some delay after effecting such union, and, finally, orgasm which is simultaneous for the male and female." [1] Except for simultaneity of orgasm, this description aptly sums up the goals and therapeutic measures developed in Masters' and Johnson's clinic. Van de Velde's *Ideal Marriage*, a particularly influential book of the 1920s, had also persuaded many couples that all these goals are normal and natural, in fact the best that any sexual relationship can offer. And yet, as Kinsey points out, most of this behavior "would be anathema to a large portion of the population, and an outrage to their mores." [2] He asserts that "perhaps a half or more of all persons" are not interested in prolonging a sexual encounter. [3] "This is true, for the most part, of the more poorly educated portions of the population, although there are not a few upper-level individuals who react similarly. It is a mistake to assume that a sophistication of techniques would be equally significant to all persons." [4]

The second system of mores, consisting of simple and direct coitus, receives some support from the sex laws: "There has been an insistence under our English–American codes that the simpler and more direct a sexual relation, the more completely it is confined to genital coitus, and the less the variation which enters into the performance of the act, the more acceptable the relationship is morally." [5] But Kinsey also points out that while members of the lower social level favor sex that is simpler and more direct, they do so because they consider it "natural" rather than moral. They "rationalize their patterns of sexual behavior on the basis of what is natural or unnatural. Pre-marital intercourse is natural, and it is, in consequence, acceptable. Masturbation is not natural, nor is petting as a substitute for intercourse, nor even petting as a preliminary to intercourse." [6] Even when they consider some instance of sexual behavior to be immoral, they assume that nature will triumph over mere morality: "They may 'know that intercourse is wrong,' but 'they expect to have it anyway because it is human and natural to have it.' " [7]

One may possibly argue that those who are less educated are simply unenlightened in matters of sex. On the other hand, they may—as they themselves think—be more in tune with certain biological needs that more sophisticated people tend to neglect. And of course, both interpretations may be right. Examining the two systems of behavior, we may find ways in which they can actually complement one another. We may also find that for many persons both systems are needed in order to benefit from the sensuous as well as the passionate, and from the different types of orgasms which we have analyzed. In isolation from the other, neither system need be considered more or less natural or basic or definitive of sexual response as a whole.

It seems desirable to assume this pluralistic approach if only because the sexuality of lower-class, i.e., less-educated, people has been so thoroughly ignored in the professional literature. And that means that their normal patterns of response have not been properly studied. Masters and Johnson admit that their original group of 382 women were far from representative of the population at large: "The sample was weighted purposely toward higher than average intelligence levels and socioeconomic backgrounds." [8] Of the 382, only 37 were drawn from a "clinic population," and of these, all had had some high school education.[9] Furthermore, before the 37 could qualify as study-subjects, they were screened for "facility of sexual responsiveness," which included the ability to masturbate to orgasm while being observed.[10]

This biased approach to sexology did not originate with Masters and Johnson. As Kinsey states: "The sexual techniques which marriage councils and marriage manuals recommend are designed to foster the sort of intellectual eroticism which the upper level esteems." [11] And later he remarks: "In general, the upper level feels that 'lower-level morality' lacks the ideals and the righteousness of the upper-level philosophy. The lower level, on the other hand, feels that educated and upper-level society has an artificial and insincere pattern of sexual behavior which is all the more obnoxious because the upper level tries to force its pattern upon all other levels. Legends about the immorality of the lower level are matched by legends about the perversions of the upper level." [12]

Leaving aside questions of morality and perversion, it is still legitimate to ask whether there may not be advantages in each of the behavioral patterns which are systematically neglected by adherents to a single one alone. Since "intellectual eroticism," as Kinsey calls it, is now recommended so pervasively in popular and sexological literature, one needs to consider the possibility that for some couples on some (or even many) occasions it is not a bit more rewarding than simple-and-direct sexuality.

The distinction between the two systems of sexual mores involves a fundamental difference between people who insist upon inhibitions as components within their sexual behavior, and those who do not. In effect, the simple-and-direct is a pattern that considers inhibitions to be a natural and indispensable ingredient in lovemaking. On the other hand, sensuous eroticism attempts to free the participants from all physical and psychological restraints upon their amatory behavior. Some people employ both patterns, or rather each on different occasions. The either/or woman, for example, is sometimes "all but reduced to simple coitus"—to use Bonaparte's words; but at other times, she welcomes voluptuous behavior with no restraints whatsoever. Bonaparte refers to sexual inhibitions as feelings of irritation or as insensitivity towards certain practices. But not all inhibitions can be characterized in this way. An inhibition may manifest itself as a vague disinclination towards a particular erotic technique on some occasion, or merely as a preference for another, more direct type of behavior. Many women report that sexual inhibitions are intermittent. For such a woman, behavior which feels right and natural on some occasions is unacceptable for purely libidinal reasons on others.

What is the basis of this variability, and why should it be the case that inhibitions are neither constantly present nor constantly absent in many women? In general, why does a pleasurable and life-enhancing activity like languorous lovemaking sometimes create a sense of malaise in women who relish it on so many occasions? It would be misleading to assume, as some sexologists do, that inhibitions may be evaluated in terms of the *degree* to which they occur—as if what matters most is the overall quantity of inhibition rather than its function in one or another context. Kinsey's methodology suffers from the fact that he preferred to ask what it is that a person has or has not done, and how often, rather than how and why it was done. I think there may be similar defects in the interviewing procedure which LeMon Clark offers:

> As a quick method of evaluating a woman's degree of inhibition, I always ask four questions: (1) Are you willing to have sexual intercourse with the light on or do you always want it in the dark? (2) Are you willing to have intercourse in various positions? (3) Is caressing of the vulva and the clitoris acceptable and pleasurable to you, or is it unpleasant and unacceptable? (4) Are you willing to caress the penis and testicles? [13]

Possibly some women can answer such questions with a yes or no that would reveal something about their sexual attitudes. But when I posed these questions to an either/or woman, she replied:

> Except for the first, these questions can't be answered with a simple yes or no. (The answer to the first is always yes—I prefer

daytime sex because I am less tired then.) The kind of sex that matters most to me leads to uterine orgasms. For this I am always on my back with my husband facing me; gentle caressing of the vulva and clitoris *is* unpleasant and unacceptable; and I definitely prefer not to caress the penis and testicles. But all these inhibitions are gone if I am aiming instead for a vulval orgasm. [Italics in text.]

A principal inhibition for human beings, and one that is relevant to the distinction between the two systems, is the need for privacy. So powerful is this inhibition that even the scientific study of sex has been thwarted for centuries by an incredible reluctance on the part of all societies to let the truth be known in this above all other areas of human experience. Women in particular have been shielded from investigation by a desire for privacy, even secrecy, which served as a sign of modesty while also providing the female with means for both seducing the male and defending herself against him. Talking of male and female alike, Margaret Mead says:

> One characteristic of human sex behavior is the insistence on privacy. This privacy may be of many types; it may be only a demand that others who share the same dwelling may not be able to observe and there may be no objections to nonparticipants hearing what is going on. In certain very rare instances, the only demand for privacy may be that nonparticipants remain at a distance and ignore sex activities. But in most human societies, sex relations are conducted in such a way as to exclude witnesses other than couples or individuals who are engaged in comparable activities.[14]

In the case of the male, it is hard to know whether the need for privacy affects the nature of sexual responsiveness in the laboratory. Some men are shy and some are exhibitionistic, and possibly their physiological responses vary accordingly. Some men might be unable to perform under scrutiny. But even so, this may not alter the characteristics of ejaculation itself. For women, however, the mere ability to have an orgasm, as well as the nature and intensity of the orgasm, varies greatly with the woman's sense of privacy and need for emotional comfort in her environment. The psychiatrist Leslie H. Farber criticizes the experimental research of Masters and Johnson because it systematically destroys the normal conditions of coital behavior. Farber condemns the artificiality of the laboratory setting and he suggests that the very presence of observers changes the character of female response. Above all, he is outraged at what he takes to be the methodological assumption that "such qualities as modesty, privacy, reticence, abstinence, chastity, fidelity, and shame could now be questioned as rather arbitrary matters that interfered with the health of the sexual parts." [15]

There may be merit in Farber's critique of Masters and Johnson. And it may even be defensible on the grounds that something as precious and elusive as sexual consummation *ought* not to be introduced into the laboratory. This is a moral, rather than a methodological, judgment; and as such, it can be argued both ways. We do wish to preserve our dearest values from all and any cold-blooded prying that may dehumanize and depersonalize them or sap their sheer vitality. All the same, doctors are given access to everything in the body, and psychiatrists flourish in secret places of the soul, without necessarily misusing their privilege. It is the methodological question that seems more interesting. For in claiming that sexual behavior, particularly the orgasmic response of the female, requires a kind of privacy which laboratory or clinical observation vitiates, people like Farber are implying that by its very nature sexuality defies direct investigation. In Freud and his followers there is much emphasis upon the innate secrecy of the female and her furtive need to keep her sexual dispositions hidden. At least by implication, they treat the quest for privacy as an instinct close to the core of all female sexuality.

As we know, Masters and Johnson have repeatedly insisted that in the laboratory a woman responds to sexual stimulation pretty much as she does outside the laboratory. According to them, the physiological processes remain the same, even though the surroundings have to be somewhat artificial for the sake of scientific observation and experimentation. If they are right, the need for privacy must be superficial, a habit that people can easily discard, not at all a basic ingredient in human sexuality.

Both of these attitudes towards privacy are essentialistic. Farber seems to think that because some women would never respond sexually in the laboratory, that anyone who does so fails to provide important information about the nature of female sexuality. This certainly does not follow. For their part, Masters and Johnson admit that they "cannot state *empirically* that laboratory reaction and private reaction are identical." [16] [Their italics.] In some cases these reactions must be very different; in fact the findings of the Fox experiments to which I have already referred may differ so greatly from the data of Masters and Johnson *because* they were carried out under conditions of privacy. Even if the need for privacy is merely "culturally induced," as Masters and Johnson say,[17] its influence upon the physiological response of many people in coitus cannot be minimized. On the other hand, even if there is an instinct for privacy, as Farber thinks, the women who insist upon it are simply women in whom that instinct operates more strongly than it does in others. Since there is no single or definitive pattern to human sexuality, we have no reason to limit ourselves to either of these unitary models.

Whenever and however it functions in sexual behavior, the need for privacy depends upon a variety of determinants. A couple making love are in a condition of physical incapacity as far as protection against enemies is concerned. Moreover, people in the grip of powerful passions are rendered vulnerable by the sheer violence of their emotions. Women in particular may lose control and become defenseless as a result of high levels of sexual excitation. Though Masters and Johnson do point out that their female subjects often experience diminished sensory acuity, there is some reason to believe that this happens more massively and more commonly in relation to blended and uterine orgasms rather than vulval orgasms. Consider the following account of a woman's behavior at a time when she was having a multiple series of vulval orgasms:

I was one of two males who on this occasion spent the night with R——— in her own home. R——— is one of the two most multi-orgasmic women I have ever met. Sexual activity occupied approximately the first four hours of the night, and was renewed in the morning. During the four-hour session, we two men took turns with R———, and at times when we were both unerect, we stimulated her orally and manually. While no one kept count, I would estimate that she experienced between 100 and 200 or-

gasms during the four-hour period. Her orgasms were quite
obviously physiological; there was no possibility of "pretending."
At no point between orgasms did she relax or fall below the level
of sexual arousal which Masters and Johnson call "the plateau
level"—with one exception.

About an hour and a half after the evening session began,
R—— suddenly catapulted herself out of bed, bolted out of the
room, and disappeared without warning or explanation. The
other male and I were utterly baffled. I surmised that she had
had a sudden cramp, or an attack of diarrhea. After a discreet
interval, I followed her out of the room. To my amazement, I
found her three bedrooms away, comforting her three-year-old
son who had awakened and cried out in the night.

Neither the other male nor I had heard anything at all. I
doubt whether I, who was R——'s active partner at the moment of interruption, would have heard a sonic boom in the
same room. But R——, at the height of a period of sexual arousal
as extreme as any I have ever seen in a woman, heard the cry
three bedrooms away through two closed doors, and responded
to it instantaneously in the orthodox maternal way.[18]

Brecher uses this anecdote to illustrate "sensitive maternal behavior" on the part of a multiorgasmic woman—an interpretation
some people may want to question. What seems more relevant,
however, is the fact that the woman could hear a call three bedrooms away, although neither male heard it, and although she
was at the height of her sexual arousal. One may infer that in her
condition there is less of the sensory disorientation which accompanies the strong emotional involvement of either a uterine or
blended orgasm. Even in the precarious context of sexual intercourse, privacy would be less important for such a woman than
for the kind of person Robinson describes when she discusses the
dulling of the senses at the onset of a blended orgasm:

One of the most amazing aspects of sexual intercourse is the fact
that all five senses become extremely dulled as the act increases
in intensity. The ability to feel hot and cold, to feel pain, or to
hear sounds becomes almost nonexistent. The eyes take on a
characteristic trance-like stare, and vision becomes constricted.
The entire mind and body are concentrated fully on the mount-
ing sexual feeling and exclude all else. In orgasm itself the

anesthesia of the senses is almost total. Indeed many people experience a temporary loss of consciousness for a matter of seconds.[19]

One would not expect a multiorgasmic woman to lose consciousness in the course of sexual activity, since each climax leads on to another. But women who do find that simple and direct coitus often results in faltering awareness are likely to protect themselves by insisting upon circumstances which involve a considerable degree of privacy. As a matter of fact, loss of consciousness is probably rare among women, and it may not occur in uterine orgasms as often as in blended orgasms; but like the relative need for privacy, it may often contribute to the differences between the two behavioral systems.

When Kinsey describes the nature of sexual inhibitions, his ideas are surprisingly ingenuous:

> Because of the widespread taboos on the subject, the contemplation of participation in oral-genital activities often results in blocked emotional responses which erupt in bitter condemnations of the partner who initiated the activity, and sometimes produce alimentary peristalsis resulting in nausea or diarrhea. This is, of course, the clearest sort of evidence that the affected individual's initial responses were positive, for it demands a blockage of a definite reaction to produce such a violent disturbance. The male, with his higher level of sexual responsiveness, is the one who is more often interested in making oral contacts, and it is the wife who is more often offended. . . . There are several instances of wives who have murdered their husbands because they insisted on mouth-genital contacts.[20]

Kinsey repeatedly cites the example of lower animals to prove that oral gratifications, as in mouth-genital contacts, are normal and natural. And indeed they are. All monkeys and apes enjoy lengthy grooming practices along with oral-genital stimulation, masturbation, and many other eroticist techniques. But when the female's drive is intense, sex is brief, vigorous, and to the point. If primatology can reveal anything about innate patterns in *human* sexuality, one may well conclude that either/or tendencies persist in many people. This, however, is a problem for future research. In the present, one can say that normative sexologists—as even

Kinsey is, for his use of terms like "taboos" and "blocked" cannot be wholly neutral—may err in assuming that inhibitions are necessarily harmful. If an erotic technique upsets a woman enough for her to commit murder, it seems naïve to tell her: "You really *do* like the idea of fellatio, but you just have this silly notion that it's morally wicked." Nausea and diarrhea are such severe involuntary reactions that they may well result from innate tendencies which are programmed much deeper than either morality or neurosis.

Nowadays, sexual inhibitions are called "hang-ups" and thought to be very undesirable. They often are. But on those occasions when they are not, coital partners may profit from accepting them as realities of the human condition. Instead of fighting her inhibitions or apologizing for their existence, a woman might sometimes do better to use them as a means of augmenting her sexual enjoyment. Accepting them as biologic cues, rather than rejecting them as mere impediments, she may find that they often tell her what she really wants out of sex. Through trial and error, a woman can discover the particular regularity which underlies the pattern of their occurrence in her experience. While sensuous eroticism may give her optimal satisfaction on a variety of occasions, the simple-and-direct approach could be preferable on many others.

In allowing this possibility, one must realize that the simple-and-direct involves techniques and sexual responses quite different from those of sensuous eroticism. If the two systems of sexual mores were not so different, or if women could easily enjoy both, there would be less inclination to choose one rather than another. The sensuous approach creates circumstances most conducive to vulval orgasms, while the simple-and-direct would seem to orient itself towards uterine orgasms, which require much less sexplay and generally result from a concentration upon coital thrusting. Many women, probably most, find that even under extremely favorable conditions they rarely if ever achieve blended orgasms. Edmund Bergler, who claims that the blended orgasm (which he calls "the vaginal orgasm") is the only normal culmination for mature females, admits that barely 10 percent of all women are gifted with this capacity.[21] And even if one had available the most advanced therapy that science could devise, one might still find that women who regularly and consistently have blended orgasms constitute a distinct minority.

This being so, it is worth investigating means by which the two systems with their two orgasmic goals may supplement each other even if they do not harmonize on any one occasion. This is a problem that either/or women confront. For not only do they experience vulval and uterine orgasms separately, but also there is often—as Bonaparte calls it—an "antagonism" between the two. Some of these women can benefit from the advice which the Chinese scholar Changsan offered. Assuming that sensuousness and the vulval orgasm are only a prelude to the passionate thrusting that a woman really wants, Changsan recommends the following technique for a loving husband to follow:

> . . . he should assume the lower position and maintain erection long enough for the partner to complete the act, and then complete the act himself with vigour when the partner reaches the climax. . . . When his partner reaches the climax, the man may resume the top position and continue the act until her parts are thoroughly wet, her voice becomes sweet, the colour of her face changes, her eyes shut, mouth closes, tongue cools and extremities relax.[22]

This is similar to a recent report from a young man who said:

> If I really want to send a woman up the wall, I give her an orgasm or two and then I get on top and fuck her as hard as I can. This seems to give her a kind of ecstasy unlike anything else. But basically I'm a very sensuous person, and I don't often do this.

One occasionally encounters women who say they never have a "vaginal" orgasm without some previous "clitoral" orgasm in coitus. Possibly such women are combining uterine and vulval orgasms, and possibly they are having blended preceded by vulval orgasms. But most either/or women are somewhat different. They generally do not have vulval orgasms in coitus, even if they have no difficulty achieving them through clitoral stimulation of an extracoital kind. For such women Changsan's advice is hardly practical. Even though the man maintains his erection for an extraordinary amount of time after intromission, he may find that the woman does not reach a vulval climax in coitus. Either she responds quickly and passionately to rapid thrusting, in which case she has a uterine orgasm; or else she finds that the sensuous foreplay which eventuates in a vulval orgasm has taken away all appetite for coital sex. It is possible that for such women the sexual drive is not qualitatively the same on all occasions, and that the separation between the two types of orgasm is a function of two types of feeling or libidinal impulse. The woman who is satisfied by vulval orgasms in foreplay may not feel the need at that moment for the emotional catharsis that a uterine orgasm provides, just as she may have no interest whatsoever in clitoral stimulation or a vulval orgasm when it is passionate coitus and uterine satisfaction that she craves. The following is a report from an either/or woman who uses the terminology we have introduced:

Qualitatively the two desires are quite different. Desire for a uterine orgasm is a languishing, yearning kind of feeling which I am sometimes able to communicate merely by looking at my husband in a special way. Physically I have to be feeling very well and wide awake. There are three or four days quite soon after my menstrual period ends when I sense this need acutely. In this period, which I think of as my estrous period, I feel more volatile emotionally, and my vagina lubricates itself spontaneously even when there is no male in the vicinity. A desire for vulval orgasm, on the other hand, takes many forms. I may start out feeling lazy, seductive, and kittenish. Or sometimes it's an aggressive, restless, peevish feeling. Or it may start with the feeling of butterflies in the stomach in anticipation of some exciting event. Sometimes even remembered embarrassment has the same effect; and often I associate this need with the desire to be comforted. If it is my husband who initiates lovemaking, I can tell which pattern I ought to be following almost at once, because a caress to my breasts or a lingering kiss will bring about a feeling of disagreeable tension and malaise if I am in need of a uterine orgasm. Yet these techniques feel erotically satisfying when I am in the mood for a vulval orgasm. The most problematic set of circumstances for me is when basically I need a uterine orgasm, but some temporary physical indisposition gets in the way. For example, if I am too fatigued, or have overeaten, then the uterine need may still preclude the possibility of vulval satisfaction, even though a uterine orgasm is, under the circumstances, impossible. On such occasions I am simply frigid.

In this report, one discovers a temporal consideration that may be highly relevant to the either/or woman's ambivalence towards inhibitions. The variations in types of sexual interest at different phases of the menstrual cycle we shall return to in the Appendix. Here, however, one should take note of the fact that the impulse towards simple-and-direct coitus seems to be greatest soon after menstruation, in a number of days that this woman calls her "estrous" period. If such timing should turn out to be statistically significant within the female population, one might speculate about a possible relationship between this kind of phenomenon and hormonal influences that underlie reproductive instincts. These instincts, assuming their existence, may be obscured by the fact that sexual desire of one sort or another continues throughout the menstrual cycle for human beings. But if these reproductive instincts do exist, they would provide a biological basis for the sexual inhibitions we have been discussing. For while these inhibitions do not restrain a woman's desire for coitus, they do prevent it from being submerged in or subordinated to a system of sensory pleasures which are not reproductive in themselves. The passionate woman who yearns for the quick and forceful penetration that belongs to simple-and-direct coitus may be duplicating the reproductive behavior that one observes in primate species as a whole. In infrahuman primates, this pattern is clearly instinctive. In human beings it may also be, even if the contrary pattern occurs frequently and in some women as their predominant mode of sexuality.

Corresponding to her distinction between the two types of desire, the woman from whom I have just quoted also distinguishes between two kinds of sexual technique:

> Although on rare occasions I have achieved a uterine orgasm with no foreplay whatsoever, usually before coitus there are at least two or three minutes of hugging, nuzzling, and deep-pressure caressing. Qualitatively this firm caressing is very different from the gentle, light caresses which precede vulval orgasm. One difference is that in foreplay for a uterine orgasm I prefer that my breasts be let alone. Both partners take part in the hugging and

firm caressing, which feels like an effort to weld two organisms into one. After a short while, I tend to go limp, and the time for gentleness begins. For me a gentle caressing of my inner thighs is almost an invariable element in the foreplay ritual leading to uterine orgasm. I always find it amazing that the erotic impact of gently caressing this area is so strong when it is a prelude to uterine orgasms, but when I am tending towards vulval orgasms the inner thighs feel no more erotic than any other skin surface. Similarly, I have noticed that if I am "in estrus," I find it very agreeable to have my uterus palpated through the abdominal wall—but this activity means nothing to me when I am less keenly oriented towards a uterine orgasm. After a minute or two of this kind of activity, intromission may follow, or else it may be preceded by a few moments of strong manual pressure on the external surface of the labia—as if to *dis*engorge the vulval tissues. Here again the degree of pressure is very different in the two types of foreplay. Gentle, rhythmic caressing of the clitoris is an invariable element in foreplay for the vulval orgasm, but in more "passionate" circumstances I find it annoying. Intromission needs to be gentle and slow, but total, so that I can enjoy the sensation of the uterus being moved by the glans penis. At this time, if a uterine orgasm is soon to happen, I invariably utter semi-involuntary, low, hollow-throated, appreciative moans. These do not occur preceding vulval orgasms, nor on the occasions when I have no orgasm. After the initial gentleness, the momentum of thrusting builds up fairly rapidly so that after four or five strokes I would agree with Bonaparte's contention that the woman loves the violence of the blows of the penis. [Italics in text.]

It is interesting that this woman reports a systematic difference between kinds of pressure. The light and delicate touch which conduces to her vulval orgasm seems to have little erotic importance in the foreplay prior to uterine orgasms. On the contrary, it may even serve as a negative factor on such occasions. When she is in the passionate mode, she requires the emotional corroboration that seems to come more readily from a tight embrace and a firm manual pressure. Both Reich and Masters and Johnson have recognized the importance of the gentle touch as a means of awakening a woman's sensuousness, facilitating the vascular engorgement of peripheral tissues, and thereby enhancing the likelihood of those muscular contractions essential for the vulval orgasm.[23] The clitoral vibrator performs a similar task in a mechanical but superhuman fashion. In covering a comparatively large area with an extremely rapid series of movements, it increases vasocongestion without applying too strong a pressure at any one place. In limiting themselves to this kind of effect, therapists like Masters and Johnson neglect the benefits that result from firmer and therefore more emphatic touch. One need only think of the closing seconds in any number of Hollywood movies to see the difference. As the camera pans out, the happy lovers about to embark upon marital bliss fall into each other's arms. They clasp tightly, their lips press hard against each other's, and their overwhelming ardor expresses itself in so powerful a pressure that it is as if they sought to merge their bodies as well as their minds. It would be anticlimactic to imagine them backing off now and titillating one another with the delicate touches which are so appropriate as well as efficacious in moments of sensuous sexuality.

But though the simple-and-direct may have its own techniques, it may also restrain or repress those that belong to the other system of sexual mores. These sensuous techniques do not always develop with genital maturation. They usually have to be learned, and they often require a reorientation in one's erotic sensibility. One need only look at any number of best-selling books to see how great is the public demand for this kind of reorientation. In using their authority to liberate such inclinations, Masters and Johnson provide a useful service. In principle, however, their therapy for nonorgasmic women does not differ very much from the kind of self-treatment which the author "J" describes in her book *The Sensuous Woman*. "J" began with a not uncommon problem in young women: she did not enjoy sex. She courageously asked questions, sought new experiences, and finally became expert in a vast repertoire of sensuous techniques. She has little to tell us about passionate sex, and some of her "sensuality exercises" may be idiosyncratic to herself. But she often reveals prerequisites that must apply pervasively throughout this mode of sexuality. For instance, as against the Victorian mandate "Ladies don't move," consider the following:

When I get sexually aroused my body just *has* to wriggle. I've always been that way. For several years I thought it was an affliction, and on dates I used to concentrate so hard to suppress that revealing wriggle that I wasn't able to enjoy fully the kissing. I had been brought up properly and there was no doubt in my mind: No nice girl wriggled.

You can only be that stupid when you are young, I suppose.

In later years when I let my body go its own natural way, I was dumbfounded to discover that my shameful pelvic wriggle was the object of much admiration in the opposite sex. It was sensuous. And men became fascinated with the desire to find out how their penis would feel imbedded in the center of that rhythmic and provocative wriggle. One man confessed to me that for several months he had a re-occurring sexual dream along those lines.[24] [Her italics.]

If it were not so sad, one might be amused at the idea of passivity turning into a *moral* issue. How absurd, one feels, that "J" or the Victorian bride should think there was anything improper in moving her body when and how she wishes to. There is, however, more at stake than just an arbitrary restraint imposed by a tyrannical society. For while the free and spontaneous moving of one's body serves as a likely prerequisite for the sensuous, it may nevertheless militate against the passionate on some occasions. Victorian mores are often explicable in terms of prerequisites for the occurrence of passion. Though neither the blended nor the uterine orgasm implies a sense of *restriction*, the uterine orgasm minimizes pelvic gestures and bodily movement as a whole. It emphasizes the receptivity of the woman—and probably her acceptance of a biological role in which she submits to the possibility of reproduction—rather than a search for sensuous pleasures.

The usual coital position, the man on top and the woman underneath, may also occur as frequently as it does because it so easily facilitates uterine and blended orgasms. A marriage counsellor remarks (in exasperation):

And some couples will say over and over again, "There is only one *right* way to have intercourse, you know," and the right way is the woman underneath, the man on top, and no manual contact.[25] [Italic in text.]

As a matter of doctrine, Masters and Johnson tell their patients to avoid the male superior position because it tends to limit ejaculatory control and thereby diminishes the incidence of female orgasm. They advocate the lateral position as "the most effective coital position available to man and woman," and report that most of their couples end up using it in 75 percent of their coital encounters.[26] The lateral position affords great freedom of pelvic movement for both male and female. For vulval orgasms in coitus, it may rightly be preferred. But for other kinds of orgasm, the more usual position has distinct advantages. The various coital positions can be analyzed in terms of social and psychological patterns of dominance-submission, as Beigel does, but they may also serve as bodily dispositions that conduce to one or another kind of orgasm.[27]

In the next chapter I shall return to the social and psychological attitudes which enter into systems of sexual response. Here we need only mention a problem characteristic of the either/or woman. On any one occasion, she often has difficulty knowing which pattern of response, which of the two systems of sexual mores, fits her momentary mood. Given the highly charged setting in which sexual intercourse usually occurs, neither husband *nor* wife may be able to determine what the woman really wants. We are back to Freud's question, *Was will das Weib?*, applied to what a particular woman may desire at a particular moment in time, the expectation being that her feelings are rarely constant. Once they have accepted the fact of female variability, many husbands are willing to adapt to their wives' preferences. But how can a man know with any assurance what they are? He cannot, and possibly this has some biological significance. As Edward Elkan remarks, the curiosity of the male, based upon uncertainty about the female's response, may have a considerable survival value for the species:

> . . . the uncertainty of the present situation where the lover cannot, with certainty, foresee to what degree his wife may respond on any given occasion, constitutes a particular and by no means negligible charm. . . . Her attractiveness is an important factor in the survival of the human race and women, uniform in physiology and temperament, may easily prove to be less attrac-

tive to men in whose sexual ardor curiosity always plays a big part.[28]

The distinction between the two systems of sexual mores may have important consequences for sexual therapy. For one thing, it may account for the difficulties which Masters and Johnson report in relation to women classified as having "random orgasmic inadequacy" (orgasm as Masters and Johnson define it occurring only rarely in either coitus or masturbation). With these women in mind they state:

> Infrequent or rare orgasmic return with both masturbatory and coital experience has defied the Foundation's current therapeutic approaches. In some cases there were detrimental interpersonal relationships that could not be altered successfully. In others there was no evidence of inherent levels of sexual tension either present or historically described. In the majority of situations, however, the cotherapists did not find an answer to resolve the problems of random orgasmic inadequacy.[29]

The plight of such women, some of whom may not be sexual failures except on the basis of a narrow and arbitrary concept of what it is to have an appropriate climax, is represented by this letter which a patient wrote to her doctor:

> Until recently I have always been perfectly happy in my sexual relationship but since [i.e., recently] I have discovered that I had never reached a complete climax. I had felt satisfied and enjoyed it enormously. At the moment of orgasm for my husband I always imagined my climax came too—evidently his immediate reaction and subsequent content and satisfaction conveyed themselves to me, and we were both perfectly happy. Occasionally I wondered if I might not feel anything more decisive, but it certainly never worried me, and sometimes, if my husband came too soon, I was very definitely conscious of being done out of something, which helped to convince me that evidently, most times, I did reach the climax.
>
> Anyway I have now definitely learnt that there is something more for the woman and it has upset my sexual life considerably. I have reached this climax only three or four times and these quite recently, and naturally we both want it to happen every

time; we both feel miserable and upset if it doesn't and each time I cannot help thinking: We have been married seven years and I have only just discovered this. I don't suppose it will come this time—and probably it doesn't.

It seems to have become such a selfish thing on my part; before, we used to enjoy it so much *together*, but now I am always worrying about my own personal physical reactions and sensation, so that, even if it does work properly, half the joy and spontaneity seems to have been taken from it. . . .[30] [Her italics.]

From this letter alone one can hardly diagnose the woman's difficulty. But it is quite possible that such persons do better to understand and accept the diverse patterns of sexuality which are native to themselves rather than assume that they are suffering from some kind of "inadequacy." The patient's problem may merely consist in a failure to recognize that at different times she wants different things. The quest for vulval orgasms is hardly desirable if it interferes with a woman's sense of joy and spontaneity; but perhaps there would be no interference if she realized that a proper climax need not be the same on each occasion. For some men and women the following advice may be more helpful than two weeks at an expensive clinic:

Dr. Lazarus: The way this goes in my practice is that women come along and say, "I am frigid." They are unhappy about this, they are depressed, and there is a lot of marital friction. When I have gone into details, the story is, "I can only achieve manually induced clitoral orgasms." I ask, "What does intromission mean to you, what does coitus mean?" They answer, "Oh, I enjoy the intimacy, I have a good emotional feeling. But the final orgasm has to be manually induced and my husband has told me that I am abnormal." Reassuring both partners is often enough to leave them happy with their pattern.[31]

For many women it is not enough merely to be reassured. Feeling in themselves a variety of sexual inclinations, they may benefit from learning how to satisfy each in its own way. Becoming expert in the simple-and-direct, and coming to understand the nature of their own inhibitions, they may discover new and interesting facts about them; e.g., how inhibitions are affected by the frequency of intercourse. There is some reason to think that daily coitus tends to lessen inhibitions, while long intervals give them greater importance and also augment the drive for passionate sex. On the other hand, the sensuous must be allowed to develop freely, if it is to flourish. With some experimentation, a woman can become the master of her complex sexual being. The need for diversity in patterns of lovemaking is strong in both man and woman. Our civilization is finally beginning to recognize the goodness of the sensuous. It must now find ways of satisfying this component in human sexuality without neglecting others that are no less important.

Chapter 6

———— ◆◆◆ ————

VARIATIONS
IN THE MALE

Throughout this book I have been arguing that sexologists are mistaken when they claim either that the female is totally different in her sexuality from the male, or else that she is extremely similar. Men and women each belong to a continuum such that some women will resemble some men in ways that are relevant to sexual functioning, while others will differ greatly from them. It is useless to say that the clitoris is homologous to the penis, just as it is unhelpful merely to point out that women have reproductive organs which men do not. For though the clitoris is in some sense homologous to the penis, one must still determine how each of them actually functions for different women and for different men. And though men do not have anything like a uterus, they do undergo experiences which may duplicate some aspects of what a woman feels in a uterine or blended orgasm.

Thus far we have used a pluralistic analysis to account for variations in the female; but possibly this kind of approach is needed to an even greater degree for understanding the male. For the female reproductive system involves two disparate sets of participating organs—related to the vulva and to the uterus—while the male has only one organ for sexual expression. His orgasm would therefore *seem* to be identical in all its occurrences; and in fact it depends upon ejaculation in a uniform way that has no analogy for female orgasms. But such uniformity can be deceptive, and one fails to understand male sexuality if one simply says that all occasions of ejaculation are in principle the same or that there is only one type of male consummation.

Although they recognize that there may be different kinds of ejaculation, both Kinsey and Masters and Johnson maintain that by its very nature the male orgasm is *basically* the same on all occasions. They also think that an orgasm occurs whenever ejaculation takes place. In saying this, Kinsey criticizes Wilhelm Reich and his followers. For they believe that not *all* ejaculations are orgasmic, i.e., that the mere occurrence of ejaculation is no assurance that the male has had an orgasm.[1] Kinsey is willing to admit that the orgasmic release of nervous tensions is possible without an ejaculation, but he denies that ejaculation can "ordinarily" occur without a preceding orgasm.[2] He asserts that "the biologist thinks of ejaculation as the product of the convulsions which result from the physiologic event commonly known as orgasm; . . . it is difficult to understand what mechanisms could produce ejaculation without a preceding orgasm."[3] With Reich in mind, he laments the confusion of thinkers who treat the term "orgasm" as if it were identical with orgastic *pleasure*. Kinsey knows, of course, that sexual satisfaction can vary tremendously from one occasion of ejaculation to another; and he specifically points out that some men derive no satisfaction at all from the ejaculatory reaction. But, he insists, this must not be taken to mean that only *satisfying* ejaculations are orgasmic. Yet that is precisely what Reich and his followers wish to maintain. Without seeming to enter into the controversy, Masters and Johnson clearly side with Kinsey. Their chapter on the male orgasm is subheaded "(Ejaculation)," as if to indicate that nothing else is relevant to the discussion.[4]

At first sight, one might think that the issue is purely verbal. Since Kinsey and Reich both agree that behavior, as well as satisfaction, varies with different kinds of ejaculations, and since both recognize that there must be physiologic correlates for such variability, it might be thought that they are merely squabbling about the use of a word—Kinsey indiscriminately extending the term "orgasm" to all instances of ejaculation while Reich wants to limit it only to responses which he considers optimal or fully satisfying. There is, however, more involved than just a verbal issue. For Reich thinks of the orgasm as a mechanism for the total release of sexual energy, which occurs on psychological and physical levels at the same time. To say only that someone has ejaculated does not indicate a culmination of this sort. It is not just a question of having pleasant experiences but also of functioning in accordance with processes that include much more than mere ejaculation. As a way of presenting Reich's argument, Lowen claims that Kinsey was talking about sexual "climax" rather than the orgasm itself.[5] For a man would reach a climax in his sexual activity whenever he ejaculated, but only on highly successful occasions would his climax also be orgasmic. According to Reich and his followers, Kinsey has failed to identify these occasions and consequently he neglects the most important elements in the sexual functioning of the male.

While the distinction between orgasm and climax does not seem felicitous, since it merely restates the idea that orgasm and ejaculation are not the same, I think the Reichians have touched upon a weakness in Kinsey's position. For once he admits that ejaculation sometimes provides no satisfaction, he makes us wonder how—on such occasions—it can actually be "orgasmic." The notion of sexual release which is built into that concept must involve psychological as well as physiological coordinates. When ejaculations are not satisfying, why should Kinsey assume that they have in fact brought about the release of nervous tension? If the Reichians can specify which kind of ejaculation is truly releasing and which is not, their criticism will have been well taken.

Before examining the kind of sexual consummation which Reich and his followers think that Kinsey has ignored, it may be useful to review the six types of male orgasm that Kinsey delineates. As one can see, they differ not only in the nature of the ejaculation itself, but also in psychological and physiological dimensions that are more than merely genital:

1. Reactions primarily genital: Little or no evidence of body tension; orgasm reached suddenly with little or no build-up; penis becomes more rigid and may be involved in mild throbs, or throbs may be limited to urethra alone; semen (in the adult) seeps from urethra without forcible ejaculation; climax passes with minor aftereffects. A fifth (22%) of the pre-adolescent cases on which there are sufficient data belong here, and probably an even higher proportion of older males.

2. Some body tension: Usually involving a tension or twitching of one or both legs, of the mouth, of the arms, or of other particular parts of the body. A gradual build-up to a climax which involves rigidity of the whole body and some throbbing of the penis; orgasm with a few spasms but little aftereffect. This is the most common type of orgasm, involving nearly half (45%) of the pre-adolescent males, and perhaps a corresponding number of adult males.

3. Extreme tension with violent convulsion: Often involving the sudden heaving and jerking of the whole body. Descriptions supplied by several subjects indicate that the legs often become rigid, with muscles knotted and toes pointed, muscles of abdomen contracted and hard, shoulders and neck stiff and often bent forward, breath held or gasping, eyes staring or tightly closed, hands grasping, mouth distorted, sometimes with tongue protruding; whole body or parts of it spasmodically twitching, sometimes synchronously with throbs or violent jerking of the penis. The individual may have some, but little, control of these involuntary reactions. A gradual, and sometimes prolonged, build-up to orgasm, which involves still more violent convulsions of the whole body; heavy breathing, groaning, sobbing, or more violent cries, sometimes with an abundance of tears (especially among younger children), the orgasm or ejaculation often extended, in some individuals involving several minutes (in one case up to five minutes) of recurrent spasm. Aftereffects not necessarily more marked than with other types of orgasm, and the individual is often capable of participating in second or further experience. About one sixth (17%) of the pre-adolescent boys, a smaller percentage of adult males.

4. As in either type 1 or 2; but with hysterical laughing, talking, sadistic or masochistic reactions, rapid motions (whether in masturbation or in intercourse), culminating in more or less frenzied movements which are continued through the orgasm. A small percentage (5%) of either pre-adolescent or adult males.

5. As in any of the above; but culminating in extreme trembling, collapse, loss of color, and sometimes fainting of subject. Sometimes happens only in the boy's first experience, occasionally occurs throughout the life of an individual. Regular in only a few (3%) of the pre-adolescent or adult males. Such complete collapse is more common and better known among females.

6. Pained or frightened at approach of orgasm. The genitalia of many adult males become hypersensitive immediately at and after orgasm, and some males suffer excruciating pain and may scream if movement is continued or the penis even touched. The males in the present group become similarly hypersensitive before the arrival of actual orgasm, will fight away from the partner and may make violent attempts to avoid climax, although they derive definite pleasure from the situation. Such individuals quickly return to complete the experience, or to have a second experience if the first was complete. About 8 percent of the younger boys are involved here, but it is a smaller percentage of older boys and adults which continues these reactions throughout life.[6]

In discussing Kinsey's analysis of the male orgasm into these six types, Lowen argues that none of them characterizes what he or Reich would call an orgasm. They are not "full" or "total" orgasms, according to Lowen, because they all reveal an inability to surrender. By "surrender" he means: "Surrender to the woman, surrender to the unconscious, surrender to the animal nature of man. . . . It involves the ability to give oneself fully to one's sexual partner without unconscious reservations." [7]

At this juncture it may be interesting to note that Marie Robinson thinks of surrender as something definitive of the female. Identifying the "central characteristic" of the human male as aggressiveness, she insists that "the essential characterological structure" of the female involves an altruistic and trusting ability to submit to his aggressiveness. The woman's orgasm is thus

a physical expression of her "sensual eagerness to surrender." [8]
Lowen would seem to be suggesting that surrender is not distinctively feminine, and in fact that all occasions of orgasmic release require it.

Even if one does postulate some kind of surrendering as a concomitant of the orgasm, however, there is nothing in Kinsey's account to rule this out. Lowen claims that tension or rigidity of the body, as in the 45 percent of all males who belong to type 2, is a defense against the giving in which constitutes a necessary condition for total orgasm. For that to happen, he says, the man must experience "involuntary pelvic movements and body convulsion." [9] By this he means rhythmic swinging of the pelvis as well as convulsions throughout the body as a whole, both occurring around the time of ejaculation. But in order for the convulsive response to exist, one would have thought that the body must already have become tense. There cannot be convulsions unless the body alternates rapidly between tension and relaxation. If a man remained rigid throughout the experience and never relaxed, this would surely indicate some pathological condition such that Lowen might argue that no real orgasm could take place. But it seems strange for him to insist that men in Kinsey's type 2—which is to say, almost half of all men in the population sample—do not have total orgasms simply because their ejaculatory response involves some rigidity. Lowen tells us that this signifies a "fear of orgasm," but how does he know? Kinsey's description gives us no reason to think that these men are all motivated by fear or that their orgasms are anything less than total.

Not only does the type 2 response look clearly orgasmic, but also type 3 would seem to fulfill the Reichian criterion of involuntary convulsions in the body as a whole. But here again Lowen claims that "rigidities, tensions, and spasm are contrary to the nature of the orgastic reaction." [10] What one would like to know, however, is whether the rigidities, tensions and spasmodic twitching undergone by the men in type 3 continue unrelieved and unrelenting throughout their coital experience. Presumably not, since Kinsey speaks of a gradual build-up to orgasm, and says that it involves "still more violent convulsions of the whole body." It is relevant here that respiration changes from gasping and breathholding in the earlier stages to heavy breathing during the orgasm itself. In the course of this intricate pattern of sexual response, there must obviously be moments of relaxation as well as tension, a releasing of bodily rigidities as well as a tensing of various muscles. Type 3 differs from type 2 in the extraordinary degree of violent convulsions which it involves. But *a priori* one feels that this alone should not be taken as a necessary sign of pathology; and in the response that Lowen recommends, there is likewise an extraordinary—i.e., statistically abnormal—violence in the bodily convulsions.

The difficulty one has in understanding what Reich and his followers are referring to as *the* orgasm—how it differs from other occasions of ejaculation and why it is preferable to them—is accentuated by the fact that they describe this wonderful consummation in terms of so many nonempirical variables. Thus not only does Lowen speak of "surrender" without telling us how one can verify its occurrence, but also he claims that only when a man feels towards a woman "love on a deeper level than words can reach" is he able to surrender to her.[11] He even says that "No man can love a woman unless he loves all women," from which it follows that only a man who is able to love womankind as a whole is capable of undergoing an authentic orgasm. For all one knows, this may be true. It is conceivable that only a pervasive capacity for love will enable a man to express his sexual feelings towards the particular woman whom he has chosen as a coital partner. But until we know more precisely what is meant by "love" in this context, very little is gained by defining the orgasm in terms of it.

Similarly, Reich really tells us very little when he defines orgastic potency as "the capacity for surrender to the flow of biological energy without any inhibition, the capacity for complete discharge of all dammed-up sexual excitation through involuntary pleasurable contractions of the body."[12] In his glossary, Reich defines orgasm as "Unitary involuntary convulsion of the total organism at the acme of the genital embrace."[13] Not only are we left uninformed about the nature of "biological energy"—despite Reich's unfortunate attempts in his days of decline—but also we are confronted with: the implausible notion that there cannot be orgasmic release unless the body *as a whole* experiences involuntary contractions; the obscure belief that sexual excitation is the kind of entity which can be dammed up; and finally, the assumption that there is something in human nature which can be described as the "capacity" for completely discharging the dammed-up excitation. Reich is not wrong in saying that sexuality involves some kind of biological energy. But he is wrong to think that this "energy" must be something more or less hydraulic, something that flows on through human experience and that people can surrender to in order to free themselves of all inhibitions. This conceptual model explains nothing, and it does ignore the fact that human sexuality always occurs within one or another system of inhibitions which create sexual energies in some respects while also destroying them in others. A biological current of a libidinal sort that flows on in its own dimension and can ideally exist without any restraints or inhibitions is simply a myth as far as human beings are concerned.

Nor can sexual excitation be dammed up or completely discharged in the way that Reich means—though one could certainly say that frustration causes an increase of tension, which may result in a more powerful discharge. As Masters and Johnson point out, male orgasms are generally more satisfying after a period of continence has allowed seminal fluid to achieve a greater volume than it does shortly after an earlier ejaculation.[14] We also know that men resemble the males of all other mammalian species in progressively losing sexual interest as a result of ejaculations that occur within a variable but fairly short period of time. In other words, there does exist a refractory period for human males during which they will be depleted of sexual energy in both the physiological and the psychological senses of that term. Even if libidinal interest returns quickly, as it does for younger men, a succession of orgasms within a period of hours tends to be less passionate from one ejaculation to the next. The later orgasms depend more on sensuous techniques and local stimulation, and possibly that is why men often feel that only the first one provides a "total release." Since they do go on to further orgasms, however, the use of the word "total" can only be paradoxical.

In talking about the complete discharge of all dammed-up sexual excitation, Reich has in mind a particular activity, a single event, in the course of which the male pulls out all the plugs, so to speak, and in one involuntary catharsis surrenders himself to his authentic being as a sexual creature and thereby fully expels all of the libidinal tensions that the universe has accumulated in him. It is not surprising that so many ingredients in Reich's definition are nonempirical. For the belief that man is so constituted that any explosion of this sort can possibly occur is surely unverifiable. Men do have orgasms which they characterize as being wholly satisfying, but these orgasms range through several of Kinsey's six types and they involve different muscles of the body in different ways on different occasions. The great majority of men do not experience convulsions throughout their entire body. If the Reichian refuses to believe that such men are *really* satisfied, the burden of proof is on him. It seems fruitless to tell people who claim to have fully satisfying orgasms that there is a secret ingredient which makes all the difference and which they have never had.

As another way of approaching the Reichian dogma, it is worth considering Lowen's distinction between "sensuality" and "sexuality." In his chapter heading he even uses the word "versus," as if to indicate their antagonism. And indeed, Lowen considers the former to be a perversion of the latter.

Except for the fact that he believes in only one kind of orgasm, and that he insists upon the normative preferability of what he calls sexuality, Lowen's distinction somewhat resembles my own analysis of the sensuous and the passionate. He thinks of the sensualist as one who is only interested in prolonging the state of sensory excitement. Such a person cultivates any kind of stimulation which will increase erotic excitation and cause it to continue as long as possible. His attitude, oriented towards pleasures of the senses, is what Lowen calls "a function of the surface only." [15] Though there are various social and characterological consequences that Lowen derives from this attitude—such as a tendency to promiscuity and homosexuality—he relates them all to the sensualist's concentration upon forepleasure as opposed to the satisfactions that come from endpleasure or "orgasm."

Lowen speaks of sensuality as a manifestation of a disturbed sexuality. In its normal function, according to him, the sexual process uses sensory stimulation as a mere preliminary to the discharge of energies and the total release of bodily tension. Summing up his position, Lowen says:

> Normally, forepleasure activities should terminate as soon as the genital organs are ready for coitus. Once the vagina is well lubricated and the penis is fully erect and charged, any delay in commencing coitus risks a decrease in the excitatory state rather than an augmentation of it. Much as one may have to give up a pleasure that is so enticing and alluring, one risks missing the boat at the other end of the voyage.[16]

But is there only one boat and only a single voyage for everyone? Lowen recognizes that the emphasis upon genital discharge, which characterizes what he calls the sexual individual, may also turn into pathological behavior. Just as the sensualist is considered perverted in minimizing the importance of genital discharge, so too does Lowen stress the abnormal implications in the behavior of men who avoid forepleasure and obtain immediate release regardless of what their wives may want. It is, therefore, only a certain kind of interest in sexual endpleasure that Lowen recommends. In doing so, he establishes a single standard of excellence, a single criterion for orgasmic success in all men and presumably all women. In effect, he is opting for the passionate at the expense of the sensuous, or rather a kind of harmonization in which the former predominates over the latter. He could justify this order of priority only if he could show that alternatives involve lesser degrees of sexual satisfaction or else pathological modes of orgasmic release. But the evidence for this is not at all convincing. Different emphases upon the different aspects of human sexuality provide different kinds of erotic experience, different kinds of bodily pleasure and different kinds of libidinal release. But *a priori* there would seem to be no basis for preferring one over another, for setting up a model that would apply to all of the diverse situations in which men and women find themselves, or for insisting that only a perfect blend of the sensuous and the passionate can provide the optimal orgasm. A man who orients himself towards the sensuous on some occasion may find that his eventual ejaculation is less explosive, and perhaps less pleasurable, than it would have been if he had shortened the period of foreplay and concentrated more directly upon genital discharge. But to tell him that he must commence coitus just as soon as his penis has become erect and his wife's vagina lubricated, assumes that we know better than he does about the satisfactions which *he* can derive by maximizing endpleasure and minimizing forepleasure. It also assumes that we are able to know what this man *really* wants, even if he thinks he wants something else.

These assumptions are both mistaken. Not only is variety worth recommending as a general principle, but also it is in the nature of sexual satisfaction that no one but the participant himself can determine where and how it should or can occur. If a man informs us that he is totally satisfied even though his orgasm was gentle rather than violent, as often happens after prolonged foreplay, who is to say that he has failed to achieve complete release? It is always possible that he has not, and after experimenting with other sexual practices, he may inform us of a change in his preference. But then again, he may have no reason to change. There is nothing in the nature of either the sensuous or the passionate that requires him to use them in any single or exclusive way. Both may be equally loving, equally a giving of oneself, equally pleasurable, and equally desirable. Each may be misused. But as long as each eventuates in a climax that the individual finds fully satisfying, neither is uniquely orgasmic. Masters and Johnson claim that with older males it may often be preferable to enjoy the lengthy period of erection that comes with aging rather than to make an effort—which in older men is sometimes futile anyhow—to bring about an ejaculation.[17] In that event, one may want to deny that their experience is truly orgasmic; but even so, the matter is more complex than the Reichians realize. For with or without ejaculation, coital experience may be wholly satisfying to these older men, and even an optimal sexual release in view of the sexuality which is being released in them.

Instead of trying to determine which configuration of the sensual or the sexual is to serve as a universal standard, or just how a false orgasm is to be distinguished from a true one, it may be more interesting to see whether the distinction between the sensuous and the passionate can be used for analyzing different kinds of male orgasm. I have already suggested that in the female different types of orgasm—blended, vulval, or uterine—may be related to differing attitudes towards the sensuous and the passionate. Since these differences in attitude apply to the male as well as the female, it would not be surprising if they contributed to different types of orgasm in him as well.

In the Freudian and neo-Freudian tradition, there is a tendency to find a parallelism between the clitoral-vaginal transfer in the female and comparable developments in the male. Whereas the young girl begins with sensitivity in the clitoris which may later turn into an unwholesome reliance upon clitoral orgasms, the young boy is thought to awaken to the possibilities of sexuality through masturbation, which can be equally harmful if it becomes a major interest once he has reached adulthood. Comparable to the vaginal orgasm would be the male's ability to engage in coitus with a libidinal satisfaction that combines the pleasures of penile stimulation with those that come from gratifying the need to penetrate the female. It is not, however, this kind of distinction between types of orgasm that I wish to perpetuate. It assumes that masturbation in the male must be infantile and it blurs precisely the distinction between different types of male coital orgasm which we are trying to understand.

As a more promising point of departure, we do better to begin with Reich's analysis of typical phases of the sexual act. For our purposes, it can be taken as particularly relevant to the male since, as it stands, it probably represents only the blended orgasm in the female. Reich himself generally speaks as if it was the male he really had in mind. His analysis follows: [18]

During the period of forepleasure, the male undergoes a pleasurable erection and then feels an urge to penetrate. The man is "spontaneously gentle." At penetration he feels none of the sensations which characteristically precede ejaculation, and neither does he wish to "pierce through" the woman sadistically. Coital friction continues to be gentle during a phase of voluntary control, consciousness being focused upon genital pleasures that result from slow and effortless movements of the pelvis. Friction may be interrupted during periods of rest, and when it is continued, it causes an ever-increasing excitation that spreads more and more to the body as a whole. There ensues a phase of involuntary thrusting during which voluntary control of excitation is no longer possible. Rapid heart beat and deep expirations begin; sensitivity concentrates upon the genitals; "melting" feelings radiate to other parts of the body, and involuntary contractions (not yet ejaculatory) take place in the total musculature of the pelvic floor. "These contractions occur in waves: the crests of the waves occur with the complete penetration of the penis, the troughs with the retraction of the penis."

From this stage on, the male's excitement increases until it reaches a sharp peak. The involuntary muscular contractions become more intense as they augment in frequency. At the acme of excitement, the first ejaculatory contractions begin. Thereafter there occurs "a more or less intense clouding of consciousness; the frictions become spontaneously more intensive, after having subsided momentarily at the point of the acme; the urge to 'penetrate completely' becomes more intense with each ejaculatory muscle contraction." Excitation becomes so extensive as to result in strong contractions of "the whole body musculature." There then occurs a release of tension and motor discharge which Reich calls "a flowing back of the excitation from the genital to the body." It is this that constitutes orgasmic gratification and eventuates with physical and psychological relaxation.

Apart from minor details, such as the fact that many men thrust deep and hold still during ejaculation rather than intensifying the frictions, this panoramic description may suitably describe what is composite and thus "typical" in the male orgasm. But in different men, on different occasions, the experience will vary in accordance with the degree and nature of forepleasure, and in general the importance which is given to the entire period of voluntary control. Reich himself suggests that prolongation of the voluntary phase "to a moderate degree" is harmless and may even increase the overall enjoyment. But what he considers to be a moderate degree of prolongation would probably seem far too little for the excitation and sensory delectation that matters so much to the sensuous individual. Similarly, the model fits the phase of voluntary control, particularly foreplay, into a pattern that requires the male to be active in coitus in a way that does not interest all men and all women on all occasions of lovemaking. The psychiatrist Theodor Reik describes a patient who insisted that the woman take the active role in sex: "She had to take the position usually reserved for the male in sexual intercourse and make all his movements. When I asked him why he refused to take the sexual role of the male, he replied, 'That's no activity for a gentleman.'" [19] Reich, like Reik, would insist that such a person must be neurotic in his sexual orientation. And undoubtedly they are right: but not because there is something in the nature of the male orgasm that requires the usual thrusting pattern in order for the male to achieve a satisfying or even total release, but only because a man who consistently and dogmatically avoids pleasurable uses of his pelvis is surely blocking out a vast segment of sexual gratification to his own detriment. The activity itself, the man submitting to the woman's ministrations, is not essentially neurotic, and neither can the culminating ejaculation be refused the honorific label of "orgasm." It is true, however, that the orgasmic experience will be *different* from what it is for the more active and aggressive male. It will be sensuous in a way and to a degree that his is not.

On the other hand, a man who concentrates upon the involuntary phases within Reich's description may be undergoing a kind of passionate experience that Reich does not adequately explain. In this pattern, forepleasure and voluntary control are minimized because excitation is already so great that a gradual buildup is unnecessary and unwanted. Reich, like many other psychiatrists, generally assumes that such men must either be sadists who wish to use the woman as a mere instrument for their instant gratification, or else premature ejaculators who fail to achieve complete orgasmic release. But in many cases in which the male abbreviates the periods of forepleasure and voluntary increase of excitation, neither of these pathological alternatives apply. The loving and wholly adequate male is often capable of a rapid and thoroughly satisfying consummation—as Kinsey also recognized when he remarked that the ability to ejaculate quickly may even be a sign of superiority.[20] Certainly a woman whose impulse is so strong on some occasion that she can tolerate few of the preliminaries of sensuous foreplay will prefer the kind of orgasmic pattern illustrated by the following report:

> I think that some women are almost into orgasm *before* you begin—although my *impression* has been (doubtless vanity) that this required a kind of appreciation of much that happens before even touching. In those cases, *I* simply went *right* to fucking immediately, and they struck me as extraordinarily (and wonderfully) overwhelmed by each thrust, certainly uncontrollably so, nearly unconscious within a minute or two—indeed, frightening me a little the first time, as if maybe she would die right there beneath me, suddenly and violently—but no pelvic movement, except for a kind of flinching at first. [Italics in text.]

This kind of passionate sexuality involves an orgasm that builds to a crescendo and then declines, as in Reich's model. But the foreshortening of the earlier phases creates a configuration different from the Reichian trajectory, just as the prolongation of these earlier phases does in the case of sensuous sexuality. By analogy with our description of female orgasms, and employing what we have said about the sensuous and the passionate throughout this book, we may therefore postulate three kinds of male orgasm: the sensuous, corresponding to the vulval orgasm in women; the passionate, corresponding to the uterine; and the blended, which the Reichian model seems to represent as a combination of the other two, comparable to the blended orgasm in women. As in the case of the vulval orgasm, the sensuous male orgasm may either focus upon the pelvis—whether in masturbation or in coitus—or else include other erogenous areas of the body as well. As in the uterine orgasm, the passionate male orgasm is doubtless related to some reproductive impulse (even instinct) which requires the deepest and most forceful penetration possible. And finally, like the blended female orgasm, the blended male orgasm would harmonize the attributes of the other two in ways that may certainly be preferable for some people on some occasions, but not necessarily for everyone at all times.

Having sketched this distinction between three types of male orgasm comparable to the three types of female orgasm, one may well ask whether in the male as in the female there are physiological correlates for such diversity. The problem seems irresolvable at the present stage of sexological science. Not only has research not been done with this possibility in mind, but also the fact that the male has one principal locus of genital sexuality, instead of two, makes it difficult for us to know how physiological distinctions may relevantly be drawn. We may eventually find that endocrinology and brain physiology are our only recourse in matters such as this. These sciences need to be developed for the understanding of female sexuality as well, but there at least we have access to considerable data that have already been provided by reproductive physiology.

The little that has thus far been done in this field does indicate that not all male orgasms are alike. Hohmann reports cases of paraplegics who ejaculate though having no *awareness* of orgasm; while others undergo the subjective experience of arousal leading to a sharp peak and sudden, wholly satisfying decline, but without ejaculation.[21] Psychiatrists sometimes encounter patients who function normally in coital situations, achieving erection, maintaining it a suitable period of time, and then ejaculating in the usual fashion, but who claim to experience no erotic arousal or sexual gratification. Not only do they fail to achieve a sense of climax, but also they would seem to escape the kind of frustration that normally results from unresolved arousal. In short, their physiological behavior is not correlated with the characteristic patterns of psychological involvement and culmination. Finally, recent laboratory investigations suggest that ejaculation has different hormonal correlates on different sexual occasions. Fox, Ismail, and their colleagues found that men who masturbated to orgasm showed little increase in plasma testosterone, although there was generally a considerable increase following coital orgasm.[22] It is interesting that these particular subjects masturbated in a context that made it difficult for them to indulge in erotic fantasies, as the masturbating male usually does, or even to enjoy the activity. The influence of these psychic conditions upon hormonal functions is paralleled by reports such as the following about LH and testosterone levels in the bull:

> Our experiments suggest that stimuli, such as the sight of a cow, and "teasing" produce a release of LH in the bull by a neuro-

endocrine reflex. Ejaculation itself was not necessarily accompanied by a change in LH secretion. If the psychological stimulus occurred at a time when the blood testosterone level was low, then testosterone secretion was increased in the following half hour.[23]

This kind of evidence is certainly sparse. But as a preliminary conclusion one may plausibly infer that those who think all occasions of orgasm in the male are necessarily alike at the level of physiological or endocrine processes must be mistaken. To say that "an orgasm is an orgasm" and therefore that sexual functions in the male are uniform and unitary in their structure is to make the same kind of error as with the female.

Given the lack of evidence about patterns in the male, it would be foolish to predict the outcome of research in this area. One can assume, however, that neither the sensuous nor the passionate nor the blended orgasm will be definable in terms of the pervasive convulsions throughout the entire body that Reich requires as the basis for distinguishing total orgasms from partial ones. This kind of physiological change, like the others that he creates by causing the subject to swing his pelvis and exhale freely, may be very helpful for patients who feel themselves hampered by a lack of muscular coordination. The inducing of convulsions may have only a limited utility; but many people can benefit from training in breathing and the use of the pelvis. Nevertheless, the results of such therapy cannot reveal the physiological correlates that we are looking for. Even if the Reichians succeed in eliciting a highly emotional climax, this special and somewhat idiosyncratic phenomenon cannot be taken as definitive of sexual consummation *as such*, or even its occurrence in all blended orgasms.

Though physiological research has so little to suggest thus far, the psychology of male sexuality offers an occasional glimmer that may be useful in distinguishing between types of orgasm. For instance, it is a commonplace in current sexology that men in the western world have dealt with women in a highly ambivalent way —on the one hand, wanting them to be sexually responsive, even provocative, and on the other hand, punishing them if they are not sufficiently modest and submissive. There has arisen the double standard which enables men to distinguish between delectable but naughty girls, who behave the way that men do, and the fine but reserved ones whom the men marry and protect as the mothers of their legitimate children. Freud described a related ambivalence in "The Most Prevalent Form of Degradation in Erotic Life," where he discerned a neurotic split between the tender, affectionate feelings that some men reserved for their wives, and the sensuous feelings that they directed towards mistresses or prostitutes. Freud was talking about a pathological condition which prevented such men from being sexually potent with their wives; but possibly his distinction applies equally well to men who are fully potent but have different kinds of orgasms with different kinds of women. Or more precisely, as a result of different attitudes that they have towards certain women. The "naughty" girl is one who engages in sensuous activities and thereby encourages the male to be sensuous towards her. As they get older, all males tend to require greater amounts of sensuous stimulation in order to achieve erection; and to some extent, Freud's patients must have been suffering from the fact that their wives had been educated to think that seductive gestures were vulgar or even immoral. But though these men could enjoy sex with their mistresses, they may not have felt an enduring passion towards them. In relation to a woman who stimulates and satisfies him sensuously, it is often difficult for the male to feel that passionate drive which comes from the need to attain the elusive female. A woman who makes it her profession to be provocative thereby defines herself as one who has nothing to withhold. On the other hand, these patients, complaining about impotence with their respectable wives, may have felt that the female they had married was just *too* elusive—as she would be if she denigrated sex or could not adjust to its changing requirements. In millions of other Victorian husbands, particularly younger ones, there may have flourished the kind of sexuality which involves adequate potency and a passionate impulse towards wives who are only partially inhibited—not extremely repressive but not especially sensuous either. In the world at large, this may still characterize a major proportion of the sexual behavior of men during their prime years.

Discussing variations in male sexuality, one must take note of the fact that in all mammalian species males respond to the cyclical changes in the female. In species that limit female sexual interest to an estrous period, the male is generally aroused by the emission of chemical substances from the female which he perceives through his olfactory sense.[24] There is some evidence, but as yet it is meager, for the idea that something comparable occurs among human beings; [25] and possibly Freud was right in thinking that the conflict between civilization and sexuality originated with man's attaining an upright posture that made it difficult for the males to smell the sexual emissions of the females.[26] Be this as it may, the fact remains that civilization has created its own erotic lures, and a woman can indicate the nature of her sexual interest through communications that make it unnecessary to emit chemical substances. A glance, a sigh, a type of clothing, a stylized way of walking or moving the body, or merely the right words in the right situation, can be just as exciting as olfactory stimulation (which civilization also provides in the form of scents and perfumery).

While one cannot separate the male's response from the female's stimulation or from the female's reaction to the male's response, masculine sexuality is somewhat autonomous. Even in primate species where the male's activity is largely geared to the female's estrous period, the male attitude is to some extent independent of the sexual state of the female. Not only is grooming a continuous sensuous interest in the males as well as the females, but also the pervasiveness of male sex drive is indicated by the fact that males will mount other males and females who are not in estrus, as if to demonstrate their permanent availability. Among the infrahuman primates, most of this activity is ritualistic, or else related to patterns of dominance; but in man the need to achieve orgasmic consummations operates as a characteristic hunger that often makes its imperious demands on a weekly and even daily basis. Since man's sexuality is so largely interwoven with the effects of civilization, however, his orgasmic response will itself vary in accordance with social and psychological forces at work within him. It serves to express individual attitudes towards the female rather than a generalized need to ejaculate.

For this reason, we can expect to find as many subdivisions

within the sensuous, the passionate, and the blended as there are male attitudes towards females in general and towards particular women on particular occasions. Something comparable also applies to types of female orgasm. There the major categories seem more discrete because they have definite physiological correlates to demarcate one from the other; but in the female as in the male, the subdivisions are equally important. And though it may only be psychological differences that enable us to distinguish between types of male orgasm, these differences can be quite remarkable. Even the man who gives himself in an ardent and forceful discharge of the passionate sort may do so in a mood of either aggressiveness or affection. The passionate orgasm in a male may be the climax to a virtual, or even an actual, rape of the female in which there is little love to match the total release which the man achieves; but it can also manifest itself in great kindliness as the male pleasures the woman with a loving and sincere interest in ecstatic possibilities for her as well as himself. On many occasions the male effects a compromise between these two extremes. On still other occasions, he may perform passionately in the sense of going through the muscular motions with dedication and a kind of ardor, while also withholding some element of his being for reasons of resentment or anger. Within the sensuous and the blended orgasms, there will be similar diversity. A man who prolongs his erection for the sake of exotic pleasures of the senses may do so either as a purely hedonic device compatible with love for a woman he wishes to satisfy, or else as a means of deriving selfish benefits without giving much of himself to his coital partner.

Homosexuals and promiscuous males of the Don Juan type differ from other men in their choice of a sexual object: either a member of their own sex or else a constantly changing member of the other sex. This difference in object choice between such men and the usual heterosexual is not an extraneous consideration, as their apologists sometimes maintain. It will have a major influence upon the individual's sexual response. It will determine the character of his orgasms, but not necessarily in a single way. The fact that Don Juan goes from woman to woman will affect his relationship with each of them, and yet there is nothing in his behavior to limit his attitude to either the sensuous or the passionate. His promiscuity may be a device for escaping passionate involvement with any particular woman, or else it may express a consuming passion that he undergoes with each of them in turn. Similarly, he may be promiscuous because sensuous pleasures continually elude him, or else because he has discovered how to renew them by endlessly changing partners in the dance of sex. And all such alternatives may belong to an orientation which is either selfish or loving, bestial or humane. Among homosexuals one finds a similar diversity.

In every male there lingers that attitude of sexual serviceability, that readiness to procreate, which seems so prominent among the nonhuman mammals. If, as Simone de Beauvoir says, women are the slaves of nature because they are the vessels of reproduction, men instinctively feel a kind of biological solicitude which makes them eager to demonstrate their virile capacities with some female or other.[27] Social ideals like courtly love, romantic love, and marital fidelity also express the male's need to serve his counterpart in the sexual scheme of things. For most men, this need is rather inconstant, and frequently it is not strong enough to override other interests. But it helps to explain that pride in performance which matters so much to so many men and which enters into the phenomenology of the homosexual as well as the Don Juan. It may also explain masculine jealousy, which cannot be accounted for on purely prudential grounds, the male fearing that his woman will not be available to him at some time in the future when he may desire her. Instead, or rather in addition, the jealous man feels threatened by the realization that someone else is doing with his mate what only he must do. To extend this analysis throughout the mammalian order would surely be hazardous, but the following anecdote is relevant even if one takes it as a reflexion of a largely anthropomorphic insight:

> In small herds of water buffalo (an important farm animal in southeastern Asia) it is sometimes found that one bull in a man-arranged harem is not able to service all of the cows. When this is the situation, the owner may bring in one or even two additional bulls. What commonly happens next is a peculiar example of male psychology. The original bull dominates the new

ones so they become entirely impotent. And he is now able to mount successfully all the cows.[28]

The male's need to consider himself an adequate performer explains his fascination with anything that will prove his virility—whether it be the size of his biceps, the length of his penis, the number of orgasms he is capable of having in a single night, or the extent to which women are receptive to him. But also it may show itself in a desire to give the woman just that kind of orgasmic experience which *she* requires. Until recently, Anglo-Saxon women used to cruise the Mediterranean because it was only there that they could easily find men whose every gesture promised a kind of sensuousness that was harder to find at home. Other men pride themselves on their ability to gratify a woman's passionate needs by a comparable ardor of their own. Doris Lessing maintains that in order for a woman to have a vaginal orgasm she must intuit a commitment on the part of the male: "It is the orgasm that is created by the man's need for a woman, and his confidence in that need. . . . There can be a thousand thrills, sensations, etc., but there is only one real female orgasm and that is when a man, from the whole of his need and desire takes a woman and wants all her response." [29]

There is some reason to believe that passionate orgasms in the female of the sort that we have been calling uterine and blended are thwarted if the woman cannot trust and admire her mate at the moment of coitus. Masters and Johnson refer to negative evaluations of the male as a "major source" of orgasmic dysfunction in women.[30] There is sufficient evidence from angry and embittered wives to indicate that *vulval* orgasms can occur with or without positive evaluations. Deutsch describes what she calls a "malicious orgasm" in which the woman's rhythmic contractions are part of a sexual "duel." [31] But if it is true that some kinds of orgasm depend upon a sense of trust and admiration, this may account in part for the enormous efforts—both sexual and social —that men have made in the course of human development to prove themselves both admirable and trustworthy.

In the attempt, they often prove the opposite. Masculine passion frequently uses an idealistic façade as a means to satisfy a momentary impulse of the body; and in general, males often confuse excellence with mere muscular superiority. Of course, this too can have its advantages. Many women value the brutishness of the male, provided it does not degenerate into brutality. Women may tolerate emotional and even physical violence if they feel that it signifies a bond which commits the male to a continuing relationship with them. But it is the man's passion they usually crave, not his sadism. Though a forceful and aggressive male is more apt to provide uterine and blended orgasms, not all aggressiveness is brutal or overbearing. In the passionate sexuality that most people cherish, the woman is never bruised or otherwise injured. In his autobiography, Malcolm X asserts that women need to be beaten from time to time—that way they know who is boss. By this he possibly means that they will admire and even trust their mate. In the world that Malcolm X knew, this might only happen if the male inflicted pain and thereby proved his physical capability despite social humiliation. He says that the good husbands who are always sweet and considerate to their wives (i.e., those who provide them with sensuous pleasures) find themselves despised and therefore flock to their favorite prostitutes on the way to work in the morning.

But no woman needs to be hurt or beaten with a stick, although many women love to be "beaten" with a penis once in a while. Lacking this, they may become disagreeable and scornful. Consider the following conversation between a patient and her psychiatrist:

> She said, "He wanted to make love to me last night. He sidled up to me and then, hesitatingly, tried to caress me. The worm! I was so disgusted, I shoved him out of the bed."

> I could feel her contempt for him, and it angered me. I replied spontaneously, "If I were your husband, I'd have beaten you up."

> To my surprise, she said, "I wish he had." [32]

One may say that Malcolm X and this patient alike make errors in judgment typical of sado-masochism. The sadist wants to inflict emotional ecstasy upon a woman, but it is something that he tries to *inflict* because he cannot induce the real thing. Convinced that he is unadmirable and untrustworthy in himself, as in fact his behavior causes him to be, he forces the woman to experience fearful emotions which simulate an actual orgasm. The masochist cooperates because even a simulation may be preferable to the total absence of emotional contact. For people with so great a need for passion, sado-masochism is no solution; but neither is sensuous sexuality, whose innocent delightfulness will merely be experienced as a sham and a superficial mockery.

❦

It is the male's concern for adequate performance, related to the fact that he possesses a natural tool for the pleasuring of the female, which also underlies the complexities of premature ejaculation. This sexual problem is more interesting for our purposes than impotence and the inability to ejaculate after an erection, since in those conditions the male deprives himself of sexual gratification whether or not he thwarts the female. In what is called premature ejaculation, the male is often functioning in ways that *only* frustrate the female. In giving a diagram for ejaculation which he considers premature, Reich assumes that the male's excitation fails to reach the kind of peak that occurs in a "normal orgasm." [33] He suggests that if a man ejaculates soon after intromission, this prevents him from experiencing coital pleasure of any sort. But *can* sexual satisfaction be gauged by reference to the duration of coitus that precedes ejaculation? On some occasions a hasty orgasm may indeed rob the male of pleasure, but frequently the man Reich would label as a premature ejaculator has a satisfying and even tumultuous orgasm. What Masters and Johnson call "the heedless male driving for orgasm" may be heedless only or primarily from the point of view of his wife. In terms of his own orgasmic drive, he may be neither heedless nor deficient. If he considers himself inadequate and seeks therapy for his "condition," perhaps he is manifesting more than anything else the typical male desire to perform in accordance with what a woman expects of him.

Very often women hope to find a mate who will ejaculate at a time that coincides with their own orgasm; and for many men, as well, this kind of simultaneity signifies emotional oneness and a proof of mutual love. Frequently it does bespeak a harmony between two persons who attune their pleasures to each other's needs and inclinations. Certainly one can savor postorgasmic relaxation better if one's partner has been fully satisfied at approximately the same time. But sexual love can express itself in many ways, and it also flourishes when orgasms are not simultaneous. Oneness can be experienced through the joy that the faster partner feels in satisfying the slower, or vice versa. There is even a sense in which lovers are more fully aware of one another when their orgasms occur at different times. Near the climax, in both male and female, the senses lose their acuity and therefore a simultaneous orgasm may prevent each partner from experiencing the other's consummatory delight. For some people, to enjoy the beloved's orgasm is as deep and intimate a pleasure as the sharing of responses that are timed in perfect unison. In an article entitled "Sex as Work," Lewis and Brissett argue that the fifteen popular marriage manuals which they have studied all treat sexual response as if it were work that had to progress according to a schedule. Mutual orgasm is treated as the product of a laborious synchronization: "Remember, *couple* effort for *couple* satisfaction! That's the key to well-paced harmonious sex play!" [34] [Italics in text.] But human beings are not clocks; they should not be expected to chime at the same moment—pleasant as that may be when it happens spontaneously.

In their discussion of premature ejaculation, Masters and Johnson suggest that it is the male's fear of performance which usually causes him to ejaculate so quickly. In *some* cases this is undoubtedly true. And if the male is dissatisfied—for whatever reason—with his ejaculatory pattern, he may possibly benefit from the kind of therapy that Masters and Johnson describe. Through the "squeeze technique" he will be able to condition himself to refrain from ejaculating; and through a reorientation towards the sensuous, he will find new ways of enjoying the coital situation. At the same time his wife will find it easier to achieve at least a vulval orgasm, which often requires lengthy stimulation. One can also say that couples who turn to Masters' and Johnson's type of therapy are the ones who are most likely to profit from it. For if the wife did relish the rapid and forceful beating by the penis, she would probably not complain of orgasmic inadequacy even if as a matter of fact she had no orgasms, or at least no vulval orgasms. Similarly, if the male refused to consider anything but his own sexual pleasure, he would not submit to therapy even though his wife was being used as an instrumentality. The couples who are likely to succeed with Masters and Johnson are therefore those in whom the male either ejaculates too quickly for his own enjoyment, or else feels distress at his inability to satisfy the female.

Having said this, however, it seems to me that there are various difficulties in Masters' and Johnson's therapy for premature ejaculation which must be subjected to further study. Even their definition, for which they apologize but use throughout, is both misleading and problematical: They consider a man a premature ejaculator "if he cannot control his ejaculatory process for a sufficient length of time during intravaginal containment to satisfy his partner in at least 50 percent of their coital connections." [35] This definition is not to apply in cases where the female partner is persistently nonorgasmic for reasons unrelated to the rapidity of the male's ejaculation. Nevertheless, there are many women who are nonorgasmic in the sense of not having vulval orgasms, and yet orgasmic in the uterine mode, or else fully satisfied in the absence of all orgasms. As a consequence of their basic theory, Masters and Johnson fail to recognize that sexual satisfaction is not identical with the having of orgasms, particularly of the vulval type. One also wonders why the figure of 50 percent has been chosen. The context in which the definition occurs would seem to indicate that the 50 percent figure is dictated by the fact that a marital unit consists of two people and that mere equity requires each of them to be satisfied at least half of the time. The same standard would seem to apply to the concept of "give-to-get" which Masters and Johnson use as a way of encouraging couples to take turns in pleasuring one another. This attitude may be highly commendable from the point of view of sexual morality and democratic egalitarianism. But it is not presented as such. Instead Masters and Johnson pretend to be advocating techniques which derive from the very nature of human sexuality. The man they define as a premature ejaculator is said to be suffering from an inadequacy and in fact an organic dysfunction, his "cure" consisting in a prolongation of erection which is considered to be more normal than a quicker ejaculation.

The difficulties in Masters' and Johnson's concept of premature ejaculation are also revealed by their account of circumstances that bring it into being. They describe the young male being "conditioned" to this pattern by as little as a single visit to a prostitute who was interested only in effecting a quick ejaculation for the sake of a rapid turnover in her trade. In other cases, they state, the male's haste in lovemaking under precarious conditions causes him to indulge in speedy coitus even after marriage. Habits of rapidity are also said to be induced by the withdrawal method of contraception as well as the double standard which convinces both husband and wife that only men need to be satisfied sexually. In all this, Masters and Johnson never seem to recognize that males may ejaculate quickly because this belongs to a kind of response which they find exciting in its vigorous self-expression and rewarding as a means of emotional discharge. In many cases at least, the fast and forceful ejaculation belongs to a passionate attitude which may or may not satisfy the woman and which may or may not be sadistic, but which authentically belongs to man's aggressive nature in a way that none of the magnificent delights of sensuousness can approximate. Since rapid ejaculation is the norm in all the other primate species, one may plausibly speculate about its being deep-rooted and even instinctive in human beings. Surely that would explain why it is that men who frequent prostitutes are willing to pay money for the right to ejaculate so fast. It would be astounding if they could be *conditioned* to this after an initial visit, as Masters and Johnson say. And neither would they indulge in the other practices that encourage quick ejaculation—male-superior position, rapid intromission, vigorous thrusting, etc.—if they didn't find it more gratifying than Masters and Johnson admit. In the course of their therapy, Masters and Johnson caution against the usual (male-superior) coital position because it impedes ejaculatory control. But since this position *is* such a common one throughout the human species, there may be something in the nature of man's sexual need which not only conduces to, but even requires, a fairly rapid ejaculation.

Far from interpreting Masters' and Johnson's therapy as one that merely enables a biologic process to function correctly, nature having been liberated from the unwarranted interference of social restraint, one may see it as itself a method of psychosexual conditioning. After the two-week period of intensive treatment, the squeeze technique must be readministered for at least six to twelve months. During this time the male is being conditioned to a slower rate of ejaculation and the female is being conditioned to vulval orgasms which are a function of his new capacity for prolonged stimulation. Both of them are being conditioned to a greater appreciation of the joys and satisfactions of sensuous sexuality. This is an educational process whose potentiality for human welfare need not be denied. But it may also entail a deflection from that ecstasy, that eager bursting forth, which only the passionate can provide.

Conclusion

———————◆◆◆———————

THE LIMITATIONS OF PLURALISM

In this book we have been studying human sexuality from a pluralistic point of view. By avoiding the temptation to assume that people are essentially alike, we have suggested various interrelated hypotheses about patterns of sexual response. These patterns are innumerable in their individual differences, but possibly they also belong to the two major systems which we have been discussing. On the one hand, the passionate attitude, which may be characterized as the need to be overwhelmed by emotions, is correlated in women with a capacity for uterine and blended orgasms that are terminative and fully satisfying. In men as well as women, the techniques that lead to passionate orgasms are relatively simple and direct, much of the libidinal drive resulting from inhibitions which may be innate as well as socially influenced. On the other hand, the sensuous attitude favors the liberated techniques of prolonged foreplay and eroticism in general. In women it conduces to vulval orgasms, which are sometimes individually nonterminative though wholly satisfying in a series. Since blended orgasms combine the passionate and the sensuous, they provide a means of harmonizing the two systems. But harmonization may vary considerably from one occasion of successful love-making to another.

Even if these ideas are substantially correct, however, I must confess that some of the most interesting questions about human sexuality have not been approached, and that problems with which we began may seem as irresolvable now as before. For instance, I originally lamented the conflict between the sensuous and the passionate, but I cannot claim to have provided a blue-print for eliminating that conflict. Harmonization between the two modes of sexuality is probably unavailable to most people on most occasions. And even when it is available, it may not always be preferable to the satisfactions that accrue without harmonization. Though we have described psychological and physiological correlates of harmonization, we have not determined how it may be achieved—or when it ought to be. It is as if we have merely been analyzing potentialities for enjoyment but letting others decide what is best.

This is not entirely true, for various possibilities have also been defended as human opportunities. And if we delineate them with clarity and sympathetic corroboration, we make them more significant to people who might otherwise ignore these pleasures or fail to recognize their availability. But even so, questions of choice may still remain no less vexatious than they have always been. Faced with the diversity of authentic responses which pluralism suggests, the reader may not find that he knows how to improve his sexual response even if he understands it better. Of course, he may not feel any need to change. Some people will continue to prefer the sensuous or the passionate to the exclusion of the other; and some will seek to harmonize them occasionally but not often, or at different times and in different ways. It is always possible that such choices may be mistaken, however, and I am not confident that what we have said thus far provides the assistance that most people will require in order to choose the life which is best for them.

We cannot escape these shortcomings merely by saying that sexology is different from moral and social philosophy. For our generalizations in one field inevitably affect our conclusions in the other. In this regard, consider Sherfey's belief that the number of orgasms attained is "a measure of the human female's orgasmic potentiality." [1] From this purely numerical criterion of what she takes to be the erotic function, related to her notions about the essential insatiability of all women, Sherfey infers that only civilization impedes free and unlimited sexual activity:

> Having no cultural restrictions, these [infrahuman] primate females will perform coitus from twenty to fifty times a day during the peak week of estrus, usually with several series of copulations in rapid succession. If necessary, they flirt, solicit, present, and stimulate the male in order to obtain successive coitions. They will "consort" with one male for several days until he is exhausted, then take up with another. They emerge from estrus totally exhausted, often with wounds from spent males who have repulsed them. I suggest that something akin to this behavior could be paralleled by the human female if her civilization allowed it. [2]

Whatever one may think of this view of human nature, it cannot be refuted by the opposite but equally extreme ideas about the social order which derive from Bonaparte's conception of female sexuality. Starting with the belief that only the "vaginal" type of woman is best adapted to the erotic function, and that this kind of woman has no need for sensuous foreplay or multiple orgasms or anything else that departs from the reproductive aspects of coitus, Bonaparte envisages the ideal female as both monogamous and socially passive, a person who defines herself in terms of home and children. This model prevailed in western civilization for many centuries. It is disappearing very rapidly. How it can be replaced by new ideals, alternatives that will enable different women to fulfill themselves in accordance with their disparate inclinations, remains as a problem for all of us.

Other problems too require further investigation. Man in the western world has created a concept of "perversion" which he needed in order to achieve the sustenance that comes from believing that there must be a right way and a wrong way in all matters of importance. Perversion is what he defines as the wrong way in sexual response. It is conceived to be "unnatural," "immature," "less than ideal" in view of innate human potentialities.

But if there is no sexual nature of a uniform sort, no unitary sexual instinct, no universal goals or culminations, neither can there be anything to warrant this concept of perversion. Sexual failure is always possible; but as sexuality may succeed in any number of ways, there is no behavior that *necessarily* perverts it. At the same time, it would be erroneous to assume that the so-called perversions are merely alternative attitudes, as desirable as any other sexual possibility. For one thing, they sometimes involve harm to other human beings, and are therefore morally wrong. The problem of choice remains, even if the pejorative essentialism has been removed.

This kind of difficulty appears most prominently in the question of homosexuality. Even Freud seems to have been unable to reach an unambiguous conclusion about it. In the famous letter to the mother of a homosexual, he insists that her son does not require treatment and should not be considered neurotic simply because his libidinal interests are directed towards members of his own sex. In articles such as " 'Civilized' Sexual Morality and Modern Nervous Illness," Freud attacks western civilization for the cruelty and stupidity with which it has tyrannized over sexual minorities in general.[3] And yet, Freud constantly affirmed that the libido has only one normal and natural goal: heterosexual coitus. In a remarkable sentence in the letter, his position appears in its total ambiguity: "Homosexuality is assuredly no advantage but it cannot be classified as an illness; it is nothing to be ashamed of, no vice, no degradation, we consider it to be a variation of the sexual function produced by a certain arrest of sexual development."[4] In speaking of homosexuality as "a variation of the sexual function," Freud would seem to be treating it as one of the ways in which the sexual instinct normally fulfills itself. But obviously that is not what he believes since he immediately ascribes this variation to "a certain arrest of sexual development." The homosexual was not to be considered ill but only because his perversion involved a condition which could be psychologically stable despite its inherent immaturity.

Neither of these two ideas in Freud is acceptable to me. The latter is just a reiteration of essentialism, and the former would seem to be a convenient compensation for the bigotry that the theory of the libido contains within itself. Freud did not go far enough in his condemnation of society's sexual intolerance. For that is largely the consequence of beliefs, which the Freudian doctrine fosters as much as any other, that nature indicates an ideal direction for human sexuality and that all who fail to live up to it must be inferior.

In rejecting essentialism, I am also rejecting the idea that heterosexual coitus has been ordained as the optimal or exclusive goal for all human beings. But from this I do not conclude that homosexual behavior is just another means, as good as any other, that people may indiscriminately use to express their sexual impulse. That is what some gay liberationists maintain in their struggle for tolerance. The struggle is justified, but the theory seems no more warranted than the heterosexual bias it wishes to condemn. As usually stated, the homosexual argument assumes that orgasms are all alike, that "the" sexual instinct is equally satisfied by every kind of orgasm, and therefore that an appropriate partner for any individual can belong to either sex. As an instinctual activity, sexual response is thought to be in principle the same whether the beloved is male or female. And this, I believe, is a fundamental error. What is suitable or unsuitable, desirable or undesirable, in the choice of a sexual object will depend upon a great many variables, including one's innate disposition, hormonal tendency, psychological development, and social conditioning. As long as homosexuality remains a minority interest for human beings, as for all other species, it cannot function as an equally viable means by which everyone may express his or her sexuality. It will always exist in a world that perpetuates the sexual needs of the majority by cultivating them in every facet of social life, by nurturing them in childhood and by facilitating their completion at maturity. This would happen even in utopia. While some people may be able to achieve their optimal satisfaction through homosexuality, most others will not.

We may argue for a society that is more sensitive to differences in sexual response, and we may encourage people to find their satisfaction through any behavior that does not harm others; but we cannot enunciate general principles that would enable an individual to choose a life which is most suitable for *him*. To do that we would need a kind of certitude about various empirical questions which no science is able to provide as yet. These are questions about innate biological and hormonal forces, psychological patterns of development, social determinants, moral consequences, and in general the human capacity for achieving happiness through one or another sexual orientation. Given the scarcity of reliable data, we can only make tentative suggestions. And no one can foresee the outcome of future investigations.

FERTILITY AND THE FEMALE ORGASM

One of the major goals of human sexuality is the reproduction of the species. This is the goal that primarily interests the biologist as an empirical scientist studying the evolution of mankind. In the course of human development, however, sexuality has also become an end in itself, a source of enjoyment that is valued for its own sake whether or not it serves as a reproductive mechanism. In the near future, medical technology will probably separate sex and reproduction even further, through better methods of contraception and more sophisticated uses of artificial insemination. But for the great majority of people in the past and in the present, sexuality has always been permeated by the realization—whether fearful or hopeful—that it is the natural and instinctive means to reproduction.

In this Appendix we shall apply some of the sexual theory of this book to several problems in reproductive physiology. The resolution of these problems depends upon empirical and experimental research; but since the agency of reproduction is sexuality, such research inevitably presupposes concepts in the theory of sex. If what we have been saying about types of orgasm is correct, new investigations are needed, and new avenues of theoretical speculation.

The following are the problems that we shall be exploring:

I. UTERINE SUCTION

In order to conceive, a woman need not be orgasmic. Nevertheless, many scientists have believed that the female orgasm enhances the likelihood of conception, and that it does so because it promotes the transport of sperm through the female genital tract. It does this, they maintain, by means of suction in the uterus which results from waves of contraction, a positive pressure changing to a negative pressure at the moment of orgasm. Recently Masters and Johnson have questioned the existence of uterine suction in human beings. In the popular literature, they are even credited with having "exploded the myth." [1] If, however, they have been studying only one type of female orgasm, one must consider the possibility that other types may indeed involve uterine suction and therefore enhance the probability of conception.

II. EXTRAUTERINE FACTORS AFFECTING THE MECHANICS
OF UTERINE SUCTION

As one of their reasons for denying the existence of uterine suction, Masters and Johnson claim that orgasms are normally accompanied by a "tenting effect" within the vagina such that the uterus is lifted out of contact with the thrusting penis. In this elevated position, the uterus would not have access to the sperm, which collect in a seminal pool on the posterior vaginal floor; and so, even if there were uterine suction, it could not facilitate sperm transport. There is, however, reason to think that the tenting effect does not occur in all women, and possibly not in all types of female orgasm. This kind of variability may also be relevant to the influence of other extrauterine factors: e.g. breathing patterns or abdominal pressure from the weight of a coital partner. Since apnea exists in some types of orgasm, whereas in others breathing is characterized by hyperventilation, one must determine whether these patterns affect the behavior of the uterus and whether they have any relationship to reproduction.

III. EJACULATORY TIMING IN COITUS

In any one coition, reproduction will be a function of the male's ejaculation as well as the female's reaction to it. If female orgasm has a positive effect upon conception, and if this effect is related to uterine suction, the woman's orgasm must occur later than the male's. Unless there is already semen in the vagina, suction cannot affect conception. The timing of ejaculation in relation to different types of female orgasm thus becomes a matter of some importance.

IV. PERIODICITY OF SEXUAL DESIRE

In most infrahuman mammals, there exists a clearly demarcated estrous period, i.e., a number of days in which the female shows maximum sexual arousal coordinated with the time of ovulation. Some women report increased desire at regular phases of their menstrual cycle. But it is not known whether this phenomenon is related to ovulation, and in general whether it has any influence on conception. In view of the ambiguities in the questionnaires that are ordinarily used, one cannot know for certain what is even meant by "sexual desire," either in those women who report that they do have something like an estrous period or in those who do not. Given the reports that are available, one must find a way of evaluating the evidence while also clarifying the relevant concepts. Neither this, nor any of the other problems, can be resolved at present. But new speculations may lead to new ways of approaching them. Section V is entitled: SUGGESTIONS FOR FUTURE RESEARCH.

I. UTERINE SUCTION

Although there are numerous references to uterine suction in the literature, Masters and Johnson deny the validity of such reports. They maintain that "there is no definitive evidence to date to support the concept of an active uterine role in aiding and abetting sperm migration from vaginal deposition sites." [2] Apart from reasoning about the mechanics of the uterine-elevation reaction, to which we shall return in the next section, they make this negative assertion on the basis of two of their experimental findings: first, that the waves of uterine contractions were observed to be expulsive, not sucking or ingesting in character; and second, that fluid placed in a cap fitted over the cervix did not move inwards as a result of orgasm. Speaking of the waves of contractility in the uterus, Masters and Johnson claim that "corpus contractions start in the fundus, work down through the midzone, and terminate in the lower uterine segment." [3] Unfortunately, the experiments which lead to this conclusion are inadequately described. We are told merely that "uterine physiology has been investigated with both intrauterine and abdominal electrode placements and acceptable physiologic recording techniques." [4] Other physiologists, aware of the difficulty of being sure that electrode readings truly indicate an expulsive quality in the contractions, have no way to check the data, since neither the data nor the methodology are presented. The second finding of Masters and Johnson results from an experiment in which a radiopaque substance, resembling semen in consistency, was placed in a plastic cap and fitted over the cervix. The liquid was not seen to move, and thus no sucking effect was observed, when X-rays were taken during and following orgasm. This experiment has been criticized by Fox and Fox on the grounds that if the uterus is comparable to a polyethylene bottle or squeeze-bulb, as there is reason to believe, putting a cap on it will interfere with its ability to cause suction.[5] One cannot create a vacuum in a plastic bottle if it is capped. The experiment seems quite inconclusive, to say the least.

It is interesting that Masters and Johnson recognize that a stronger uterine contraction is correlated with a more intense emotional release on the part of the study subject: "Inevitably, the degree of excursion of recorded corpus contractive response parallels the study subject's subjective and the observer's objective evaluations of the physical and emotional intensity of the orgasmic experience." [6] And yet, paradoxically, they assert that masturbatory orgasms seem to be associated with stronger uterine contractions than do coital orgasms:

> Although the number of experiments is not sufficient to allow an empirical position, it is current belief that the corpus contraction patterns initiated in response to automanipulative techniques are of greater intensity and duration than those resulting from coitally induced orgasmic experience. Certainly it is subjectively true that study subjects report that usually the experience with orgasm induced by masturbation is more intense than, although not necessarily as satisfying as, that resulting from coition.[7]

It is hard to believe that a masturbatory orgasm would normally provide greater "emotional intensity" than a coital orgasm—at least, one can hardly imagine this to be true outside of a laboratory setting. If a woman feels self-conscious during coitus, perhaps because she is being observed, a coital connection may well be less emotional than it would be under normal circumstances. One must also distinguish, more clearly than Masters and Johnson have, between physical and emotional intensity. Masturbatory orgasms are often physically more intense than coital orgasms in the sense that they may involve stronger contractions of the orgasmic platform together with augmented readings of several other physiological indices. But, under normal circumstances, masturbation is generally less intense as an *emotional* outlet than coitus with a spouse or loved one. Under the contrived and somewhat artificial conditions of the laboratory, the emotionality of coitus may be inhibited while the effects of masturbation remain constant. In that event, subjects could very well report a greater intensity, even emotional intensity, for their masturbatory as opposed to their coital experiences *in the laboratory*. The only way to ascertain the inhibitory influence of human observation is for couples to make physiological recordings free from supervision by anyone else. This is what Fox and Fox did, and, as I have pointed out earlier, their data and their conclusions contradict Masters' and Johnson's.

If it were the case that uterine contractions during coitus had no effect upon uterine suction and sperm transport, women would differ drastically from most of the lower mammals. Uterine suction has been observed in the work of many researchers. In the technical literature, no one has challenged the findings of Hartman and Ball on rats, of Evans on dogs, and of VanDemark and Moeller on cows. Although uterine suction has been observed in other orders of mammalian species as well, for our purposes it will suffice to mention these three. The methodology of the studies on the rat and the cow are similar. Clamps called hemostats were quickly applied to the horns of the uterus following coitus in such fashion that no sperm could subsequently pass from the proximal to the distal portions. Hartman and Ball found that if they killed the female rat 30 seconds after ejaculation, and clamped both horns prior to 63 seconds after ejaculation, then no sperm were found distal to the clamps, although many appeared lower in the uterus.[8] However, if they killed the rat at 1 minute after copulation and clamped the horns prior to 2 minutes, then sperm were found distal to the clamps on both right and left sides. Sperm motility alone could not possibly account for the distance traveled in such a short time. VanDemark and Moeller worked with locally anesthetized cows rather than dead ones while they applied the clamps, since they wanted to obviate the possible effect of slaughter on sperm transport. When clamping was achieved a mere 3.3 minutes after coition, sperm were found as far along as the ovarian portion of the oviduct.[9]

Evans' work on dogs involved a fistula or hole near the oviducts in the uterus, the fistula being stitched to an opening in the animal's external hide. Evans found that semen spurted out through the fistula at about 25 seconds after ejaculation. By their own motility, the sperm could not have traveled that quickly. Evans concludes:

In considering factors responsible for the rapid transport of spermatozoa through the uterine horns of the dog, the two most probable appear to be antiperistaltic movements of the uterus and the alternately increased intra-abdominal pressure brought on by the straining of the female during "orgasm" as witnessed by the writer. Each straining was followed by the appearance of more sperm suspension at the fistula opening. . . . Sperm suspension introduced into the vagina [artificially] resulted in no recovery of sperm from the fistula openings even 1 hour 40 minutes afterwards. This the writer considers as supportive evidence that there is some nervous reaction on the part of the female dog during "orgasm" which aids materially in the propulsion of sperm suspensions up the uterine horns.[10]

It has often been stated that in the lower mammals females have no orgasms. Ford and Beach, for example, assert that, with the possible exception of the domestic cat, positive indication of a sexual climax has not been detected in females of any infrahuman species.[11] But probably differences in definition account for the discrepancy in reports. Evans evidently refers to the antiperistaltic (or ingesting) uterine contractions accompanied by abdominal heaving when he speaks of orgasm in the dog. Ford and Beach, however, seem to be referring to vulval contractions, since they state that orgasm in human females is greatly facilitated by the stimulation of the clitoris during intercourse. They account for the lack of orgasm in lower animals by the fact that their coital positioning does not conduce to clitoral stimulation:

> . . . clitoral stimulation is minimal or lacking when coitus is accomplished by rear entry, the habitual position employed by all primates except our own species. These items of information lead to the interesting but highly speculative hypothesis that orgasm is rare or absent in female apes and monkeys because their method of mating deprives them of one very important source of erotic stimulation.[12] *

It seems unlikely, though by no means impossible, that the mechanism of uterine suction which functions effectively in so many lower mammals would be abandoned in the evolution of mankind. And yet various physiologists have, by means of a speculum or an artificial phallus, watched the cervix during female orgasm and found no movement of the mucus in the cervical os.[15] But once again, the definition of orgasm may be of crucial im-

---

* In the years that have elapsed since Ford and Beach wrote their book, field studies have indicated that gorillas and orangutans do not limit themselves to the dorsal position.[13] In both of these species, face-to-face coitus occurs, but it is not yet known whether the female has vulval contractions in this or any other position. Kinsey does report, however, that he has seen a female chimpanzee masturbate to orgasm.[14]

portance. Some orgasms, e.g., vulval orgasms resulting from either masturbation or coitus, may involve no movement of mucus even though uterine and blended orgasms do. These latter orgasms, which the physiologists could not readily have had access to in the laboratory, might duplicate the patterns of uterine suction found in lower mammals.

There is also experimental evidence to indicate that the human uterus can and does contract in such fashion as to produce suction under certain noncoital conditions. Working with two anesthetized hysterectomy patients, Egli and Newton found that if they administered the hormone oxytocin and thereby caused strong uterine contractions, inert carbon particles were transported from the vagina to the Fallopian tubes within 34 minutes, whereas one would expect the sperm to take at least 45 minutes by their own motility.[16] It is likely, in view of the animal studies already cited, that the particles were transported within seconds after the oxytocin injection; but since women cannot be operated on as hastily as rats and cows, the exact moment of transport could not be identified. Egli and Newton ligated the tubes, rather than using a clamp, as soon as the uterus was exposed. Of course, there is always a possibility in experiments of this sort that the surgical manipulation prior to ligation might cause a spreading of the carbon particles, instead of their being transported by uterine contractions. That this possibility is at least doubtful in this particular experiment is indicated by the fact that the tubes of a third patient, a forty-one-year-old woman, yielded no carbon particles under the same circumstances. The "oxytocin response" (i.e., uterine contractions in response to oxytocin injections) is known to be totally lacking in postmenopausal women, and this woman's age could account for the lack of effective contractions in her case.[17] It is also possible that the lack of carbon transport might have been related to the fact that she was diabetic and had aborted three months prior to the operation. In any event, the fact that her tubes were free of carbon particles indicates that the surgical procedure *as such* did not necessarily spread the carbon to the tubes of the other women.

In animal experiments generally, it has been found that uterine behavior varies considerably among individuals within a single species. Even sheep do not all evince the same degree of uterine contractility in coitus. Lightfoot and Restall found that thirty minutes after coition, five ewes did and three did not yield sperm in the Fallopian tubes.[18] Possibly one can surmise that these five ewes were orgasmic in the sense in which Evans' dogs were, and that the other three were not.

It is only by assuming that human females can undergo more than one type of orgasm that we can explain why it is that Fox, Wolff, and Baker recorded a pattern of uterine contractility quite different from that depicted by Masters and Johnson. In their uterine-pressure experiments, Fox *et al.* found that the pressure changes were minimal during male orgasm but increased markedly during female orgasm to a positive pressure of 40 cm. H_2O, followed by a sharp fall after orgasm to a negative pressure of 26 cm. H_2O.[19] Thereafter the pressure rose slowly over the next minute, during which time the uterus was relatively quiescent, and then the regular contractions returned. The negative pressure following female orgasm indicates the possibility of a squeeze-bulb kind of behavior on the part of the uterus that might eventuate in an insuck of the cervical mucus with its entrapped spermatozoa. In the one recording, presumably typical, which Masters and Johnson publish in their first book, the ultimate level of pressure within the uterus is higher than the preorgasmic level.[20] At no point is there a pattern of negative pressure following a strong contraction. From this they could only infer the absence of any suction, whereas the Foxes argue that the pressure differential which they repeatedly measured would indicate that the squeeze-bulb type of suction does occur.

Not only does the squeeze-bulb analogy of the Foxes explain their data, but also it may even be consistent with the data of Masters and Johnson with respect to the direction of the contractile waves. No matter how gently it is pressed, a squeeze-bulb will first expel some quantity of air (or fluid) and then, when the bulb is released, a comparable amount will be ingested. However, if the squeeze-bulb has two additional escape hatches, i.e., the Fallopian tubes, then a mild squeeze or contraction may yield no mucus movement at all at the cervical entrance. Vulval orgasms may involve contractions which are too weak, or else coordinated in such fashion as to render suction impossible. On the other hand, a severe contraction—one which forces the uterine walls against each other and holds them clamped together for a moment or two—could, when relaxed totally, draw fluid in through the cervix. Perhaps it does not matter which direction the contracting waves take. Perhaps what is necessary for suction is merely an intense, pervasive clenching of the entire womb. And that may simply require orgasms of a sort that Masters and Johnson never observed for the methodological and conceptual reasons that we have already discussed.

It is noteworthy that both Reich and Masters and Johnson think of strong uterine contractions as being a problem for some women. Reich says:

> The inhibition of the vegetative impulse, however, may be found in a spasm of the uterus. In such a case, the uterus can be felt on careful palpation as a well-defined, spherical mass. It is a matter of vegetative hypertonus of the uterine musculature; with the development of the orgasm reflex the mass disappears. It even happens occasionally that the mass appears and disappears repeatedly during one and the same session.[21]

Masters and Johnson state:

> The physiologic definition of uterine muscle contraction patterns during orgasm offers a possible explanation for the clinical complaints of cramping distress initiated during orgasmic response and experienced by many women (particularly multiparas). The orgasmic contractions of the corpus also have been reflected subjectively as painful stimuli in many instances by postmenopausal women.[22]

It is quite possible that *how* the uterus contracts—the manner in which its movements are coordinated—will determine whether the resulting strong contractions are experienced as agreeable or disagreeable. A state of relaxation in the muscles of the surrounding pelvic viscera may also be important. But whether this is so, no one knows. As Masters and Johnson remark, the study of the physiology of the uterus is still in its infancy.

At present the prostaglandins, especially the prostaglandins-E, are being researched as possible agents in promoting the uterine contractions of coitus. These are hormones which are found in human semen, and which, in small doses, cause the uterus to contract. In larger doses they cause it to relax and become unresponsive.[23] Thus one might suppose that prostaglandin-E could help to account for the Fox, Wolff, and Baker data in which initially the uterus contracted strongly following ejaculation, but soon afterwards became relaxed and quiescent. This particular hypothesis, with respect to the Fox *et al.* data at least, is exploded by the fact that a condom was used throughout their experiments on intrauterine pressure, and consequently the semen never came into contact with the uterus or vagina. Moreover, it has been reported in the *British Medical Journal* that the uterine suction of one Jamaican woman's orgasm was strong enough to pull a condom off the penis and leave it wedged in the cervical canal:

> A colleague of mine in Jamaica was consulted by a young woman who said that the previous night she had had condom intercourse with a soldier, and that on completion the condom was missing. The doctor did a speculum examination and found the blind end of the condom firmly held in the cervical canal.[24]

Such data would seem to be evidence against the notion that uterine suction depends primarily on semen-prostaglandins.

On the other hand, prostaglandin-E, or something very like it, has been shown to be emitted when a rat diaphragm is electrically stimulated.[25] Prolonged diaphragmatic tension is one of the characteristic features of the apnea occurring in both uterine and blended orgasms. It is conceivable that prostaglandin-E from the tensed diaphragm could help to bring about the squeeze-bulb pattern of the uterus. *If* prostaglandin-E is responsible for the uterine behavior shown in the Fox recordings, the hormone must come from a source other than semen, and the diaphragm undergoing apnea in the course of either a blended or uterine orgasm *might* be such a source.

II. EXTRAUTERINE FACTORS AFFECTING THE MECHANICS
OF UTERINE SUCTION

In the course of their argument, Masters and Johnson claim that the sheer mechanics of coitus make the uterine suction of sperm impossible for human beings. They claim that orgasms are normally accompanied by a "uterine-elevation reaction" which prevents the uterus from having access to sperm. In the orgasms they observed, Masters and Johnson found a "tenting effect" within the vagina resulting from a movement that raised the uterus out of contact with the penis and therefore rendered it incapable of seminal suction. Even if it were able to suck inwards, the uterus could not ingest the sperm since the semen collects in an anatomical basin on the posterior vaginal floor.

According to Masters and Johnson, the uterus starts to rise in the excitement phase and reaches its maximum elevation in the plateau phase, descending only after orgasm has occurred. To the woman herself, the tenting effect often has a marked influence upon her coital sensations:

> Before the orgasmic platform in the outer third of the vagina develops sufficiently to provide increased exteroceptive and proprioceptive stimulation for both sexes, the overdistended excitement-phase vagina gives many women the sensation that the fully erect penis (regardless of size) is "lost in the vagina." [26]

On the basis of this evidence and the evidence cited in the previous section, Masters and Johnson conclude not only that uterine suction is a mechanical impossibility but also that female orgasm cannot increase the likelihood of conception. For other reasons, also deriving from the mechanics of coitus, they argue that orgasm may even be an impediment to reproduction. They advise women whose vagina has been stretched by childbirth to terminate sexual behavior prior to the orgasm on occasions when they are trying to conceive. They point out that the orgasmic platform can serve as a retaining wall for seminal fluid only if it remains intact: if there are vulval contractions, the platform is dissipated and the semen is more likely to drain out. The orgasmic platform, being a thickening in the walls of the outer third of the vagina as a result of vasocongestion, loses its capacity to retain the sperm once the orgasmic contractions have reduced the vasocongestion.

From all this one may certainly conclude that *vulval* orgasms do not further conception and may even hinder it. By its very nature, the vulval orgasm may serve no direct reproductive function apart from enhancing the pleasurability of sexual encounters. What we must now determine is whether the mechanical impediments which Masters and Johnson cite occur in the other types of orgasm as well. The argument about the dissipation of the orgasmic platform through vulval contractions would not apply to the uterine orgasm, since that type of orgasm is not accompanied by vulval contractions and may not even involve an orgasmic platform. And possibly the tenting effect does not occur in either the uterine or the blended orgasms—or at least, not in every instance of them.

That neither the tenting effect nor the uterine elevation reaction can be universal in all orgasmic women is clear from Masters' and Johnson's discussion of the retroverted uterus. They remark that no elevation takes place in women who have retroverted uteruses. They merely say "there is no physiologic explanation" for this lack of elevation; and they do not inform us how coital experience is affected in these women.[27] In their sample, almost 12 percent of the women studied had retroverted uteruses. In the population at large the percentage might well be higher. Furthermore, it would seem that the tenting effect, and therefore uterine elevation, cannot occur in women who actually feel the contact between the cervix and the thrusting penis. As mentioned earlier, Kinsey reports that many women find that "the cervix . . . must be stimulated by the penetrating male organ before they can achieve full and complete satisfaction in orgasm." [28] Robinson, and others who seem to be describing blended orgasms, also say that contact with the cervix contributes to the orgasmic pleasures of women.[29] Since the uterine orgasm depends upon cervical jostling, it presupposes that the uterus does not elevate itself out of reach. The "beating by the penis" which Bonaparte describes cannot occur, or at least it cannot be enjoyed, if there is nothing there to be beaten—i.e., if the penis, instead of being felt against the cervix, is "lost in the vagina." [30] One may conclude that women who undergo the sensations that belong to all uterine and some blended orgasms must differ substantially from those in Masters' and Johnson's sample. It is quite possible that the tenting effect and the uterine elevation reaction occur in the latter but not the former.

It is also possible that the processes of uterine elevation and descent occur in patterns more complicated than those that Masters and Johnson have described. Speaking of the uterus returning to its preorgasmic position, they say that "early in resolution uterine descent progresses rapidly. However, final return of the cervix to full apposition with the posterior vaginal wall frequently takes as long as five to ten minutes." [31] In the case of women who have vulval orgasms followed by uterine or even blended orgasms, it is conceivable that the uterus elevates itself and then descends prior to the terminative orgasm. This would help to explain the orgasmic efficacy of vigorous thrusting *after* the occurrence of a vulval orgasm. As mentioned earlier, some women report that they never have "vaginal orgasms" without first having "clitoral orgasms." This sequence of events, which might be called the Changsan order after its earliest proponent, may plausibly be assumed to depend upon the fact that the penis buffets the cervix as the latter is descending after having been elevated in the vulval orgasm. The following report is consistent with this interpretation:

> On occasions when a vaginal orgasm follows a clitoral orgasm, the timing is important for me. If my husband commences vigorous thrusting immediately after a clitoral orgasm (which in my case is normally extracoital), I cannot respond with a vaginal orgasm. But if he waits until my heavy breathing has subsided, and until I have a relaxed sensation of "afterglow" in my lower abdomen, the vaginal orgasm sometimes does occur.

There is no reason to think that the subjects of Masters and Johnson employed the Changsan order, and many women who are sexually responsive, in the sense of readily having vulval orgasms, would feel no need for it. In women who do have vulval orgasms prior to their uterine or blended orgasms, it is possible that the vulval orgasms relax the abdominal muscles in such fashion as to render the woman receptive to vigorous thrusting. This would indicate a biological function over and above the enhancement of sexual pleasure.

Variability in coital behavior is also relevant to other extra-uterine factors which may affect the mechanics of uterine suction.

Several researchers have recognized that respiration may influence intrauterine pressures. As Hartman says in arguing for this hypothesis: "The abdominal and thoracic cavities form a hydrostatic unit in which negative and positive pressures are transmitted equally in all directions." [32] That one or another pattern of breathing may encourage uterine suction has been suggested by Belonoschkin among others.[33] And W. H. Cary cites an example of uterine suction that would seem to have resulted from "a very deep sigh":

> I had been frustrated by a problem in which postcoital studies indicated failure of a vigorous semen to invade apparently normal mucus in the wife. I proposed to introduce and hold this semen within the cervical canal for a short period and then remove it for microscopic study. While I was maintaining gentle pressure, the patient suddenly indulged in a very deep sigh, whereupon the semen suddenly disappeared from the cannula and did not respond to immediate reversal to negative pressure. The seminal fluid evidently passed the internal os, for the patient experienced uterine colic requiring hypodermic therapy and rest for a few hours at a nearby hotel.[34]

The woman in question conceived and delivered a normal child at term.

Sobrero tried to follow up this suggestion by having one hundred women inhale and exhale "as forcibly as possible" while he watched their cervical mucus.[35] He found that in these women the mucus was unaffected by such breathing. But since inhaling and exhaling as forcibly as possible is entirely different from a deep sigh, this experiment is inconclusive. In a sigh the inhalation is slow, and may often include a momentary apnea at the peak, particularly if a woman stretches her shoulder muscles while she sighs. One cannot know whether the woman in Cary's observation underwent apnea, but there is every reason to think that her breathing was not forcible. On the other hand, women who are instructed to breathe "as forcibly as possible" would never think of inhaling slowly and holding their breath when the lungs are full. With the instructions provided, they would be inclined to approximate the hyperventilation which accompanies a vulval orgasm; and since suction does not occur in vulval orgasms, one may assume that this kind of hyperventilation causes no movement of the cervical mucus. Finally, even if women *were* told to sigh slowly and deeply with apnea at the apex, they could never duplicate all the factors involved in a sigh which was not willed but rather arose spontaneously and involuntarily. In short, Cary's suggestion has not been, and possibly cannot be, properly tested.

Apnea is worth considering not only because it could well have occurred in the sigh we have been discussing, but also because it is a pattern of breathing that increases pressure upon the walls of the uterus. This external pressure would naturally increase internal pressure, which would augment the possibility of suction or ingesting by the uterus once the pressure disappeared in the course of exhalation. Apnea could have this effect in one or another way: either because breathholding causes the diaphragm to be raised, in which case there will be greater tension exerted by the abdominal walls upon the uterus; or else because the diaphragm descends when the lungs are full of air, as they would be just before the coital climax, and thereby amplifies the pressure in the abdominal cavity. In either event, the tensed diaphragm may act as a stiff wall against which the uterus would receive the maximum of mechanical stimulation from the thrusting penis.

Since apnea occurs in uterine and blended orgasms, but not in vulval orgasms, it is worth noting that this kind of respiratory pattern has some analogy in the coital behavior of infrahuman primates. Female gorillas and chimpanzees sometimes scream during coitus; and for that to happen, their diaphragm and also their crico-pharyngeus muscle must remain tense for as long as each scream continues. Although there is an obvious difference in decibels between screaming and breathholding, the mechanics of respiration with respect to the diaphragm and the crico-pharyngeus are extremely similar.

That uterine and blended orgasms may belong to patterns which affect uterine suction is also indicated by the fact that the coital position they usually employ is one in which the male exerts pressure by his weight and by his movements. In the male-superior position, external pressure would increase intrauterine pressure in ways that could eventuate in uterine suction. Fox and Fox point out that "pressure upon the abdomen by the hand, or in the coital situation by the male lying on the female, increases intrauterine pressure by some 10 cm. H_2O." [36] Some women find that pressure from either of these sources is particularly agreeable and erotic during the three or four days of enhanced sexual desire which sometimes occurs in the postmenstruum, and which we shall be discussing later in this chapter. Since the weight of a man feels good at such times, a woman is more apt to welcome the male-superior position in this relatively fertile period of her menstrual cycle. Changing position immediately after her blended or uterine orgasm, she would lessen the weight pressing against her abdomen and would therefore promote a pressure differential before and after the occurrence of orgasm.

There may not be a single tactic or a single mechanical procedure which conduces to all cases of uterine suction, and it may not always happen in the context of uterine and blended orgasms; but its occurrence on *some* occasions seems sufficiently likely as to warrant further investigation.

III. EJACULATORY TIMING IN COITUS

If one assumes that uterine suction occurs in human beings, and if it is related to the female orgasm, it must take place after the male has deposited sperm in the vagina in order for the process to facilitate conception. For the uterine contractions of a blended or a uterine orgasm to aid in transporting sperm, there must already be sperm near the cervix available for transport. One way of assuring this is for male ejaculation to trigger off the female orgasm, which seems to have occurred regularly in the instances of blended orgasm recorded by the Foxes. The detumescence of the penis after ejaculation consistently preceded those terminative orgasms which involved the succession of positive and negative pressures in the uterus. The Foxes describe this postejaculatory kind of orgasm as follows:

> With the final contractions of ejaculation, the male begins to relax his hold and become inert. At this point a compulsive abdominal and vaginal straining and heaving begins in the female.

The penis seems to be pushed into the vaginal outlet, and the shaft is gripped just below the glans by the muscles at the vaginal outlet, until the glans is made to form a tight-fitting plug in the vagina. At this stage the heaving reaches its maximum intensity and heralds the orgasmic contractions in the vagina and uterus at intervals of approximately 1 sec. . . . The vaginal contractions alternate with inward heaves, which carry with them a sensation of inward suction, though the intensely pleasurable orgasmic sensations are more allied to the contractions and the sense of relief these bring. The sensation of suction does not usually accompany clitoral or extracoital orgasm . . .

During the vaginal contractions, and possibly as a result of them, the penile "plug" is ejected from the vagina and coitus is terminated. Active withdrawal by the male rarely takes place. Following an orgasm of this kind, the vagina feels "closed" and very averse to further coital interference.[37]

Zumpe and Michael report that, in a group of thirteen female rhesus monkeys, three showed comparable behavior:

At the end of ejaculation, these females moved away from the males so vigorously that they collided with the side of the cage. After this, apparently involuntary pelvic movements continued for a few seconds with the female in the sitting position before the beginning of grooming by one or the other animal.[38]

Though the primate data may be interpreted in different ways, the behavior of the three monkeys resembles the human behavior not only in the occurrence of pelvic movements and ejection of the penis, but also and most significantly in the fact that both occurred after the male had completed his ejaculation.

Even in the sample of rhesus monkeys mentioned here, the percentage of females who reacted to ejaculation in this fashion is quite small. And among women as well, those who evince such behavior are probably in the minority. For most women the orgasm is less violent; and a great many women, as Theodor Reik has also remarked, find it enjoyable to retain the detumescent penis quietly within the vagina after coitus.[39]

In both kinds of women, the increasing tension in the female during coitus may itself be a factor which triggers off the male ejaculation prior to the occurrence of the female orgasm. In several primate species, the female has been observed to clutch and grasp the male during coitus in ways that have been interpreted as inducements to his ejaculation. In the sample of rhesus monkeys to which I just referred, the clutching reaction occurred as a function of sexual tension. In their report, Zumpe and Michael say:

> In females with regular access to males, the clutching reaction invariably occurred during the ejaculatory mount. However, in females denied access to a male for many weeks, which exhibited many invitational gestures, the clutching reaction occurred very early in the mounting series before the male was ready to ejaculate. This caused an abrupt cessation of thrusting as though the male were unable to continue and, when this occurred repeatedly, the female was attacked.[40]

It is as if the male rhesus felt constrained to ejaculate as a result of the female clutching reaction, but could not do so if it occurred too soon after he began pelvic thrusting. The attacks on the female would thus seem to be a mechanism for deterring the female from reaching a sexual peak before the male has had a chance to ejaculate.

In human beings similar timing may have been established by the fact that women are generally slower in their sexual arousal than men. In the case of the uterine orgasm, women may have developed faster responsiveness as a means of keeping pace with the fairly rapid ejaculation which seems to be characteristic of men in general. Whether the male's ejaculation sometimes triggers off the uterine orgasm, or the female's tension triggers off the ejaculation, or possibly both, there always exists the possibility that even in an orgasm as quick as the uterine type the male may ejaculate too quickly. Kinsey states that "for a not inconsiderable number of males the climax may be reached within less than a minute or even within ten or twenty seconds after coital entrance."[41] A minute would barely suffice to produce a uterine orgasm even in a highly responsive female, particularly since the first few thrusts need to be slow in order to keep the woman from tensing her abdominal muscles in a way that would defeat orgasm. Ten or twenty seconds would be insufficient for almost all women unless the male were able to continue deep thrusting for more than a half minute after ejaculation. On the other hand, the ejaculation cannot be delayed too long after the beginning of coitus if the uterine orgasm is to facilitate reproduction. For there would be no utility, as far as conception was concerned, in a uterine or any other type of orgasm which preceded the actual deposition of semen. From this point of view, the male-superior coital position takes on a biological significance that seems to be ignored by those who lament the fact that it is the least conducive to ejaculatory control. For if the male-superior position does make it difficult for the male to delay ejaculation, it thereby makes it more likely that the sperm will be in the vagina prior to the uterine orgasm. Thus there may be some functional basis to the fact that many women who have uterine orgasms prefer the male-superior position, and sometimes even consider it the only one that feels right for such consummations.

When Kinsey discusses the timing of ejaculation, he too recognizes that rapidity may be quite normal as a biological phenomenon:

> . . . it is to be emphasized that in many species of mammals the male ejaculates almost instantly upon intromission, and that this is true of man's closest relatives among the primates. Students of sexual activity among chimpanzees, for instance, report that ten to twenty seconds is all the time which is ordinarily needed to effect ejaculation in that species. Far from being abnormal, the human male who is quick in his sexual response is quite normal among the mammals, and usual in his own species. It is curious that the term "impotence" should have ever been applied to such rapid response. It would be difficult to find another situation in which an individual who was quick and intense in his responses was labeled anything but superior, and that in many instances is exactly what the rapidly ejaculating male probably is. . . .[42]

These comments about timing in coitus may serve to continue our discussion of the two systems of sexual mores described in Chapter 5. The simple-and-direct approach shortens the interval between intromission and ejaculation, just as it shortens the period of foreplay. Perhaps this procedure, including many of the inhibitions which it entails, serves a biological purpose. For the passionate and highly excited male is more likely to ejaculate outside the vagina if the woman fondles his penis, or kisses him at great length, or lets him caress her too extensively. Female inhibitions towards these techniques would therefore tend to increase the number of occasions in which the sperm are delivered where they are needed for reproduction rather than being spilled prior to intromission.

But as libidinal drive declines in the course of aging, eroticist techniques become increasingly important if there is to be any sexual activity at all. The uterine orgasm in the female, as well as tumultuous thrusting and quick ejaculation on the part of the male, depends upon youthful energies which gradually decline as a person goes through middle age. Older men need the sensuous techniques in order to achieve erection and even to ejaculate; older women need them because, as their estrogen declines, they no longer feel spontaneous inclinations towards uterine orgasms. The sensuous predominates in this period of life because without it sex would probably disappear. Correspondingly, Kinsey's data show that the sexuality of the socially lower-level males tends to wane earlier in life than that of the higher-level males. Since it is the lower-level males who favor the simple-and-direct, it is not surprising that their approach should be relatively unable to cope with the physical decline that accompanies middle age. But sensuous sex can last indefinitely for both male and female; and some women have been known to have a *first* vulval orgasm in their seventies.[43] One may also wonder whether many of the middle-aged men suffering from "secondary impotence" (a pattern of erective failure in men who have previously functioned adequately) are cured in the Masters and Johnson clinic mainly by a change of mode from the simple-and-direct, which served them well enough when they were younger, to the sensuous, which they now require for their sexual expression and which the clinic systematically encourages.[44]

In the prolongation of sexuality into and throughout the later years of middle age, there may be some biologic utility. For it means that the species will have access to the maximum number of reproductive opportunities. On the other hand, there are biological disadvantages in having aging males sire the next generation. They are poor risks as fathers, or at least they were so in the primitive world in which our reproductive instincts were formed, since their vitality is relatively low and they are less able to protect their progeny. Casual or passionless males are also poor risks, such men being less inclined to stay with the mother and child. It may not be merely coincidental, therefore, if the younger woman's uterine orgasm does not function with these mates as it would with more suitable prospects. Even when their thrusts are deep and their manner simulates passion, her timing may be such as to precede the moment of ejaculation in either the aging or the casual male, and this would negate the conceptive advantages the uterine orgasm might otherwise provide.

A deterrent to conception could also be instituted by the occurrence of vulval orgasms rather than those that have a more reproductive function. This would encourage the young and fertile female to enjoy the phenomenon of sex while reserving her reproductive occasions for men who are more likely to support a family. With them she could undergo orgasms of a kind that tend to enhance the likelihood of conception. And possibly it is some such pattern which explains the paradox that Malinowski describes in his account of Melanesian sexuality.[45] Although the Trobriand women were sexually liberated from an early age and wholly promiscuous prior to marriage, it was only after they settled down to a life of monogamy that they began to conceive. Without using contraceptives at any time, they seem to have acquired habits of sexual responsiveness that facilitated first birth control and then conception. One would like to know whether their success partly depended upon a systematic shift from one type of orgasmic response in youth to another in maturity.

IV. PERIODICITY OF SEXUAL DESIRE

Under this heading, there are two problems, closely related but in need of separation. First, one must determine whether there is a period of heightened desire within the menstrual cycle. And second, one must study the relationship between such a period—

assuming it exists—and the time of ovulation. This second problem is itself complicated, however, by the fact that ovulation does not occur in all women in a regular and reliable fashion. There is also the possibility that it can sometimes be induced earlier than usual as part of a woman's response to coitus. To determine the relationship between desire and ovulation is therefore to speculate about several variables, and with respect to human beings at least, the evidence about some of them is so sparse as to constitute a problem in itself.

In the females of most lower mammals, sexual receptivity is limited to a period of estrus during which coitus is normally timed to eventuate in the fertilization of the ova. In other words, sexual behavior (and, one might also say, sexual desire) is correlated with ovulation in the females of most mammalian species. In women, however, desire often occurs at times when ovulation is unlikely, and therefore one can speculate about a relationship between the two only after having studied each of them independently: first, sexual desire as a phenomenon that may or may not be cyclical; and then its possible correspondence with ovulation.

I have already quoted one study-subject who said, "There are three or four days quite soon after my menstrual period ends when I sense this need [the need for uterine orgasms] acutely. In this period . . . my vagina lubricates itself spontaneously . . ." That this report is typical of a sizable segment of the female population is indicated by Cavanagh's recent survey of the literature on rhythm of sexual desire in women.[46] With one exception, the twenty investigators he cites recognize that for many women there is a peak in sexual desire occurring soon after menstruation. Half of these authorities maintain that there is also another major peak during the premenstrual period, and some maintain that this peak is stronger than the other.

If there is a premenstrual peak in sexual desire, one might expect an increase in the frequency of coital activity during this period. But in a statistical reworking of several relevant studies, W. H. James has recently shown that there is no evidence of any premenstrual peak in coital rates. He speculates that this discrepancy may result from "premenstrual tension being mistakenly interpreted as sexual desire." [47] Tinklepaugh had earlier differentiated between *qualities* of desire during the premenstrual and the postmenstrual periods. He suggested that the period of heightened "sex desire" which falls just before (or before and during) the first days of menstrual flow is in reality a period of increased affectivity of a nonsexual sort, while the postmenstrual peak is one of true sex desire:

> Two college-trained women who were unaware of the nature of the information I sought, described a period of increased affection just prior to and at the onset of the flow. At that time, in the words of one of them, she "craves to be petted and loved by her husband" but was without sex desire unless stimulated. Her statement was verified by her husband. The observations of three other women and the reports of three husbands concerning their wives, covering periods of from four months to a year, indicated that in the absence of other stimulating circumstances which arouse desire, there was a period of increased affection without conscious sex hunger, falling variably just before or before and during the first days of the menstrual flow. These same women were aware of heightened affectivity in addition to sex desire during the postmenstrual week. Two biologically trained women kept daily records of both physical and psychologic changes over periods of four months and a year respectively. In the first one desire was at its height between menstruation and the fourteenth to sixteenth days in the four twenty-three to twenty-nine day cycles. Exuberance or physical well-being showed a high correlation with sex desire. "Affection" in this subject was at low ebb during menstruation and reached its maximum between days nine and sixteen. It then waned rapidly to reappear during the last three to five days of the cycle. The second of these subjects, somewhat critical of my designation of the premenstrual emotional state as affection, describes her feeling at that time as one of dependence. She states: "At that time I am dependent. If I have anyone about who will act as a leaning post, I lean. It looks like affection, I suppose, but it is quite selfish. As long as things run smoothly I am good tempered. But if I have to do things I don't want to do, or if anyone displeases me, I have a dreadful time being reasonable, patient, or polite. I would hesitate to call this condition affection, though when in the company of loved ones it would certainly seem like it, even to me." The affectivity

which follows the flow, which continues until approximately the midinterval, and which is correlated with sex desire "is much more trustworthy. It weathers small storms better. It does not notice things that immediately prior to and at menstruation become unbearable." . . . During the four premenstrual days, many women suffer both depression and physical distress, coincidentally with the affectionate period. This psychophysiologic state is one of the determinants of their affectivity.[48]

Since premenstrual affectivity may often eventuate in coitus, Tinklepaugh argues that whatever the coital rate may be in the days before menstruation, it cannot be taken to indicate enhanced sexual desire:

In the case of man both male and female are highly stimulable sexually. With them demonstration of affection has developed, perhaps by individual association or conditioning, so that it readily leads to sex stimulation and coitus. This stimulability of man accounts for the frequency of sex relations during the premenstrual affectionate period. Furthermore, in their retrospection and reports, women commonly determine the periods of desire by the occurrence of coitus. For these reasons it is apparent that in an organism as highly stimulable as man the occurrence of coitus is not adequate evidence of heightened sex desire.[49]

In Cavanagh's survey the sole exception among the authorities was John Money. He makes reference to only one peak of sexual desire, the one that occurs just before menstruation. He may also recognize another peak after menstruation, but it is only the premenstrual one which he takes to be truly characteristic of sexual desire in women. If one examines his use of language, however, one discovers ambiguities which may very well explain why it is that he differs from the other authorities. Speaking of the single peak, he says:

Allowing for individual variation, the consensus of opinion has been that sexual desire *in the active sense of taking the initiative* has been strongest at the progestinic phase of the cycle [i.e., preceding menstruation], that is, around the time of menstrual flow.[50]

Elsewhere he remarks:

> Androgen in females is a libido enhancer; it increases the *momentum of sexual initiative as compared with the receptive submissiveness* characteristic of estrogen in women.[51]

I have italicized the crucial words in these sentences because they indicate that Money limits the term "sexual" to the behavior of women who are "active" and who "take the initiative" in a sexual encounter. But there are many ways in which a woman may express sexual desire, and it is hard to know which of them should count as being active or taking the initiative. As I have suggested, women undergoing a uterine orgasm move around less than those who aim for vulval contractions. They tend to keep their pelvis still and relaxed, even though many other muscles of their body are tensed. Does this mean they are not being *active* in Money's estimation? And if this coital pattern gives them precisely what they want out of sex, are they or are they not manifesting "receptive submissiveness"? Is a woman who elicits male interest with a significant glance or tone of voice taking the initiative? Or must she make overtures in the form of caresses and physical gestures? The system of inhibitions which often precedes uterine orgasms might very well preclude these maneuvers as inappropriate to the sexual occasion. If, however, the woman does take the initiative in some overt manner, either before or during coitus, is she necessarily motivated by sexual desire? The kind of questing after affection which Tinklepaugh mentions can be more demonstrative, and yet less libidinal, than the subtler but equally provocative behavior that Money correlates with the level of estrogen in women. His remarks are suggestive but too imprecise.

The same kind of terminological unclarity seems to underlie Sherfey's conviction that women as a whole are "maximally potent" only during the ten to fourteen days before menstruation. She states:

> It has long been realized that sexual arousal tends to occur more readily during the luteal phase of the menstrual cycle. Kinsey et al. demonstrated this correlation statistically, indicating that roughly 90% of American women prefer relations during the luteal or premenstrual phase.[52]

Examination of the Kinsey text discloses no basis for the 90% figure, which Kinsey himself never mentions. In fact, what Sherfey says seems to be a misrepresentation of Kinsey's data. His general conclusion was the following: "Evidently the human female, in the course of evolution, has departed from her mammalian ancestors and developed new characteristics which have relocated the period of maximum sexual arousal *near the time of menstruation*." [53] [My italics.] Kinsey does not say "prior to menstruation," as Sherfey would have us believe. The actual data are these: 59% of Kinsey's sample of women noticed that there was a monthly fluctuation in their vaginal lubrication during erotic arousal. They also noticed that the time of maximum lubrication (during erotic arousal) was almost always the same as the time of maximum erotic responsiveness. By studying the time and quantity of secretion in the vagina, Kinsey could therefore gauge the time of maximum erotic response in the 59% who reported fluctuations. His findings were as follows: [54]

No fluctuations in secretion or
    erotic responsiveness 41%
Of the other 59%:
  Premenstrual increase ....69% = 41% ⎫ of the
  Postmenstrual increase ....39% = 23% ⎬ whole
  During-menstruation increase ....10% = 6% ⎪ sample
  Mid-cycle increase ....11% = 6½% ⎭

As Kinsey points out, the figures for women who report fluctuations total 129% of 59% because some of the women reported that the increased secretion occurred both before and after menstruation. If one subtracts the extra 29% from the 39% who show a postmenstrual increase, this would leave a total of 10% who experienced heightened erotic responsiveness only in the postmenstruum. Possibly it was in this way that Sherfey inferred that "roughly 90% of American women prefer relations during the luteal or premenstrual phase." There is, however, nothing in these statistics to justify any such inference. Only 69% of 59% (i.e., 41% of the total) report a premenstrual preference; and as for the extra 29%, Kinsey did not indicate how it is to be distributed among the premenstrual, the postmenstrual, and the mid-cycle categories.

Women who are not using oral contraceptives generally have an augmented amount of mucus in the vagina for a few days during their follicular phase (i.e., preceding ovulation). Hartman has referred to this cyclical phenomenon as "mucorrhea." [55] The additional quantity of mucus originates from the cervix and is present in the vagina whether or not the woman has been erotically stimulated. Masters has identified another kind of secretion, a "sweating-type reaction" of the vaginal walls which begins within seconds after the start of "effective sexual stimulation." [56] He has not observed any increased cervical secretion during sexual response, but at the time of mucorrhea cervical mucus would already have accumulated in the vagina prior to foreplay. Mucorrhea could therefore provide lubrication for coitus on some occasions at least; and the women in Kinsey's sample who reported a solely postmenstrual peak may have done so because of the enhanced lubrication resulting primarily from cervical secretion. Women who reported a solely premenstrual peak may have found that vaginal secretion resulting from erotic stimulation during the luteal phase more than compensated for the absence of cervical mucus. Those women who reported postmenstrual as well as premenstrual peaks may very well have had augmented lubrication for different reasons in the two periods.

It is possible that in some women sexual arousal increases during the luteal phase because they are aware that it is relatively safe as far as contraception is concerned. Sherfey offers a different explanation. She attributes enhanced desire during the luteal phase to the fact that the pelvic tissues are normally more congested then: "Because of the higher luteal base line of congestion, women are in a mild state of sexual excitement throughout this period, although it is rarely recognized as such." [57] Elsewhere in her book she says: "An inability to achieve multiple orgasms, a reduced intensity of orgasmic sensations, and the capacity for only manually induced orgasms at all times other than the luteal phase may be considered normal." [58] This last statement gives some clues about what Sherfey means by "sexual excitement." As we have noted, multiple orgasms are vulval in character, blended and uterine orgasms being terminative. Moreover, if an orgasm is manually induced, it must be vulval. Manually induced blended and uterine orgasms are probably impossible. Consequently, one may infer that for Sherfey sexual excitement is defined as the desire for vulval orgasms. And it may very well be the case that during the luteal phase these are more intense, less dependent upon manual stimulation, and more likely to occur in a multiple series than at any other time. Similarly, women may then prefer sensuous sex and feel themselves emancipated from the gamut of inhibitions which determine the simple and direct approach.

The vulval orgasm depends upon congestion induced in the vulval area, particularly in the orgasmic platform. As Sherfey suggests, the greater congestion during the luteal phase is surely a factor which disposes women toward sex at that time. But since the statistics indicate a significant variability in periods of heightened responsiveness, one may wonder why the higher base line of congestion does not have a similar effect on women who do not report a premenstrual peak. The reason *may* be social or psychological, some women having failed to acquire the liberated and somewhat sophisticated taste for sensuous sex; but it may also be biological, since the shift from estrogenic dominance to progestagenic dominance causes many changes besides increased vasocongestion. That this shift is relevant to sexual desire is revealed by several of R. P. Michael's experiments on rhesus monkeys.[59] In the female of that species, sexual desire wanes as soon as progesterone is added to the existing level of estrogen. Sherfey herself recognizes that something similar occurs in women who favor the postmenstrual period. She suggests that the existence of this small minority (as she takes it to be) indicates "how recently luteal phase hypersexuality must have evolved."

Since vaginal lubrication and erotic responsiveness are linked, one might be surprised that the estrogenic dominance during the follicular phase should cause mucorrhea in so many women and yet fail to enhance sexual desire in those who prefer the premenstrual period exclusively. Possibly there is less mucorrhea in women whose hormonal balance tends towards androgens or progesterone. And perhaps there are determinants of an extrabio-

logical sort as well. As one may speculate about social or
psychological factors counteracting the higher base line of congestion during the luteal phase, so too should one consider the
possibility that women who have only a premenstrual peak may
be influenced by social or psychological factors which discourage
the kind of sexuality induced by estrogenic dominance. They may
be neglecting the methods of sexual enjoyment appropriate to
the postmenstrual period. The sexual limitations which Sherfey
mentions as "normal" at times other than the luteal phase may
reflect the failure of sensuous sex in a period of the month that
requires an acceptance of inhibitions if one is to get the maximum satisfaction.

It is also possible, even likely, that differences between premenstrual and postmenstrual preferences are determined primarily by
hormonal variations among different women. Premenstrual preferences may result from a comparatively high level of androgens
in some women, while a high enough level of estrogens may pre-
dispose others towards a postmenstrual peak. In either event,
constitutional differences in the amount of progesterone would
also influence libidinal expression.

If we now try to determine the relationship between desire and
ovulation, we must begin by recalling that only 11% of the 59%
in Kinsey's sample who showed any fluctuation reported increased desire at mid-cycle. Yet, if human beings had an estrous
period comparable to that of lower mammals, one would expect
a higher percentage of women to report enhanced desire shortly
before ovulation—which typically occurs at mid-cycle according to
most authorities. But Kinsey's figure agrees with the work of
Davis, who found that only 8½% of women who reported fluctuations preferred mid-cycle, and of Hart, whose figure is only
6%.[60] These three investigators used different criteria for deter-
mining the occurrence of sexual desire, but all three of them suffer from a similar ambiguity in their methodology. If a woman is
asked to report about erotic feelings experienced at some time in
the past, there is likely to be a confusion between her memory
of desire preceding intercourse and remembered satisfaction as

a gauge of what she *really* felt. This difficulty is unrecognized or ignored by virtually everyone who has relied upon questionnaires for information about sexual desire. Though he does not seem aware of the problem, Cavanagh by-passes it in research that he accomplished with a sample of 30 women who were in psychotherapy and were "not having a sexual life." [61] Cavanagh required abstinence as a condition for his investigation on the grounds that "sex activity would drain off sexual tension and do away with any peaks." [62] This reasoning seems very tenuous since it assumes that sexual desire manifests itself most graphically in the context of privation. It seems likely, however, that women who are abstinent would often ignore the existence of sexual desires, or even suppress them entirely. In any event, many sexually active women do recognize peaks of libidinal interest which are not eliminated by coition.

In his chosen sample, Cavanagh found that the greatest number of women "stated that they had increased sexual desire on the thirteenth day, a day on which ovulation could be expected." [63] It is interesting that Stopes, the only other investigator to describe a major peak at mid-cycle (as well as a premenstrual one), was also studying women with no access to a mate—in this case, wives separated from husbands on military duty.[64] Since similar reports are not made by the vast majority of women who have coitus regularly, one can only conclude that something which happens at mid-cycle may cause an increase of desire in women who have no coital activity.

This something may possibly be the phenomenon called mittelschmerz, which some women experience recurrently at mid-cycle. Mittelschmerz causes tension or discomfort, and even when there is no pain a woman's attention may be directed towards her reproductive organs. Mittelschmerz also gives rise to sexual dreams, which Cavanagh used as a principal index of heightened libido. It is conceivable that abstinent women would interpret this condition as the feeling of sexual desire. Since women who are sexually active often find that coitus during mittelschmerz is painful or disagreeable, they would be more likely to disassociate the tension of mittelschmerz from sexual impulse. Feelings which focus attention on the sexual organs are often interpreted in widely divergent ways. As with the premenstrual-postmenstrual controversy, one needs a sharper analysis of what is meant by "sexual desire" in order to make sense of the conflicting data.

If one accepts the reports that locate the peaks of desire at times other than mid-cycle, and if one assumes that ovulation typically occurs at mid-cycle, one would have to conclude that women do not have anything analogous to an estrous period. But the evidence about ovulation is such that some investigators, at least, have questioned whether its occurrence is typically limited to mid-cycle. Virtually everyone agrees that coition in the premenstrual period is typically nonreproductive; but there is reason to think that coitus soon after menstruation may lead to conception earlier than mid-cycle. As far back as 1927, Dickinson worked at this problem by surveying various studies of conception resulting from "isolated coitus"—i.e., coitus limited to a single 24-hour period during the entire menstrual cycle.[65] Superimposing graphs based on nearly 4000 cases, he found a high level of conceptions from isolated coitus during days 6 to 11 with a peak at the 8th day. Noting that direct observation of the ovaries shows that ovulation generally awaits the 13th or 14th day, Dickinson states: "The chief puzzle in human reproduction . . . is the gap between the highest frequency of isolated fruitful coitus and of ovulation according to laparotomy evidence." [66]

One might argue that sperm remain viable in the female genital tract for a considerable length of time, but there is no good evidence that they can survive for five days. According to Hartman, sperm remain motile in the female reproductive tract for a maximum of forty-eight hours, and several hours earlier they become too feeble to fertilize the egg.[67] Furthermore, Dickinson's findings are matched by the data of McCance, Luff, and Widdowson, who report that for both single and married women there was a high incidence of "sexual feeling" during days 7 to 14 with a slight peak on day 8.[68] These investigators analyzed elaborate day-by-day entries in the diary-type records of 167 women for 780 complete menstrual cycles. This work was done more than 35 years ago, but there are no subsequent studies that would lead one to question its reliability. It is remarkable that these researchers should have found a high incidence of sexual feeling throughout much the same period as the one in which Dickinson found a high level of conceptions from isolated coitus. Whether or not the corresponding peaks on day 8 are statistically significant, their occurrence at that time may not be merely coincidental.

Hartman has criticized most of the studies which Dickinson used because, as he says, the investigators "based their conclusions on one-day furloughs from the German army in the First World War. The women who were interviewed in the obstetrical clinics were expected to recall the exact day of the menstrual cycles when their husbands had visited them 9 months before." [69] Hartman's argument does not seem very convincing. No woman would be likely to specify an exact day unless she routinely circled in her calendar the dates on which her menstrual periods began, which is precisely what millions of women have done ever since a missed period was first taken to signify pregnancy. The reported days are probably as reliable as many other questionnaire answers which have been credited with scientific accuracy. Furthermore, Hartman elsewhere acknowledges that a later study of 416 cases showed essentially the same results: an ovulation curve skewed strongly to the immediate postmenstrual period with the peak at days 7, 8, and 9.[70] As against such evidence, Hartman prefers the "well-controlled" series of studies by various physicians who were successful in overcoming infertility problems in numerous women. All of these studies argue for a concentration of ovulation days mostly within 3 days of the middle of the menstrual cycle.

While the evidence seems to be contradictory, it is also possible that both series of reports are correct. The coital pattern of a soldier with his wife on a 1-day furlough is undoubtedly different from the coital pattern of an infertile couple who keep trying vainly for conception. Having only a day together under the precarious conditions of wartime, a soldier and his wife are likely to be more vigorous and more passionate than an infertile couple in whom repeated disappointments may affect both emotions and behavior. In general, when coital stimulation is relatively mild— of a sensuous nature rather than the "beating by the penis" advocated by Bonaparte—ovulation may be unaffected by coitus; but sufficiently intense coital stimulation during the postmenstrual period, when the follicles are ripening, may possibly induce early ovulation. Clark and Zarrow associate the high fertility rate following the rape of women with the fact that in rape thrusting is likely to be more intense than in most other instances of coitus. They speculate that "this increased intensity could be an important factor in producing ovulation under these circumstances." [71] In the uterine and blended orgasms, thrusting is also forceful. Rape resembles the conditions for these orgasms in other ways as well: the male is on top of the female; the female may scream or gag, both responses entailing diaphragmatic and cricopharyngeal tension; the emotional reaction on the part of the female is usually extraordinary.

This line of reasoning is coherent with Linzenmeier's findings about the relative frequency of fertile as compared to nonfertile instances of rape.[72] Using his data the menstrual cycle can be divided into four segments: from day 1 through day 6 there were 12 cases of fertile rape and 42 cases that were nonfertile; from day 7 through day 9 the ratio reverses itself, there being 11 fertile cases and only 4 nonfertile; from day 10 through day 18 there were 53 fertile cases and only one nonfertile; thereafter to the end of the menstrual cycle, there were only 3 cases of fertile rape and 42 cases that were nonfertile. Not only is there a sudden shift towards fertility between the 6th and 7th day, but also it is noteworthy that on the 7th, 8th, and 9th days the fertile cases were almost three times more numerous than the nonfertile. These statistics tend to corroborate the other data about conception curves approaching a peak early in the follicular phase. They show that coition may be reproductive several days before the expected date for spontaneous ovulation, and they give one reason to think that vigorous coitus on an occasion that involves strong physical and emotional reactions can hasten the rupture of a ripening follicle. In this connection, it is highly relevant that Bickenbach, Döring, and Hossfeld found that 6 out of 11 women ovulated early when subjected to thermal stimulation of the cervix between days 6 and 11 of the cycle. Increase in pregnanediol excretion, taken to indicate ovulation, started 1–2 days after the stimulus was applied.[73]

Recent experiments with rats provide further evidence for the possibility that coitus-induced ovulation may sometimes occur in an animal which normally ovulates spontaneously. Relying on histological data, Aron, Asch, and Roos found that with rats which routinely ovulated every 5th day (i.e., with a 92% probability of regularity), coitus one day earlier than their normal estrus hastened ovulation in fourteen out of twenty rats or 66%.[74] These fourteen rats are not typical, however, since most female rats are not receptive to the male unless they are in estrus. Moreover, it was found that all the rats which had 4-day rather than 5-day cycles showed no ovulatory response to early coitus unless they were given a priming dose of estrogen (a dose low enough to have no noticeable independent effect on the follicles). Zarrow and Clark have published several papers on coitus-induced ovulation in the rat, but hormonally their animals were altered so drastically that one cannot be sure that their conclusions apply generally.[75] They maintain that in the rat coitus-induced ovulation is "a function of the intensity of vaginal and cervical stimulation."[76] They even find that vigorous deep thrusting with a glass rod is more effective than natural coitus for inducing ovulation, provided the operation is carried out with suitable intensity, even violence. They state: "The failure of others to obtain LH release in response to stimulation with a glass rod was probably due to their failure to stimulate adequately."[77]

Extrapolating from their rat experiments, and extending their speculations about the consequences of rape, Clark and Zarrow argue that "a certain percent of all women can and do ovulate in response to coitus."[78] Among other things, they use this possibility to explain the well-documented cases of failure of the rhythm method of contraception, and also the fact that women have been shown to ovulate at very atypical times of the month.

As the next step in this investigation, one needs a laboratory study of coitus-induced ovulation in some of the species of non-human primates which are sexually receptive throughout the menstrual cycle. One would particularly like to know whether the intensity of coital thrusting is an important factor in hastening ovulation, and whether the emotions of the female have a contributing effect.

By way of conclusion, what are we now to say about the periodicity of desire in relation to human fertility? In the great majority of women, there does not seem to be a correlation between desire and spontaneous ovulation at any phase of the menstrual cycle. However, if it turns out that coitus-induced ovulation occurs not infrequently in women, there may be something analogous to an estrous period in the sense that an appropriate type of coitus can often induce ovulation at a time when sexual desire is high. Hartman presents evidence to the effect that mucorrhea precedes the other signs of ovulation which are used routinely in the clinic.[79] For example, the peak of mucorrhea precedes mittelschmerz by two days, and the basal body temperature change by five days. The mucorrhea curve is already high at day 8, and it covers the postmenstrual period of enhanced desire. Thus, in the human female, the period of mucorrhea may be the time when increased desire is coupled with the ability to reproduce.

V. SUGGESTIONS FOR FUTURE RESEARCH

If the hypotheses implicit in this Appendix and in this book are correct, future research may disclose that women who report a maximum of sexual desire during their follicular phase are in general the ones most interested in uterine orgasms and in simple-and-direct techniques, whereas women who have a maximum of sexual desire during their luteal phase are those who favor vulval orgasms and feel inclined towards sensuous eroticism. There may or may not be times of the month which are most conducive to blended orgasms. Unfortunately, no reliable data about all this can be derived from any of the questionnaires which have thus far been formulated.

By distinguishing between the characteristics of female sexuality during the premenstrual and the postmenstrual periods, we are in effect analyzing the concept of sexual desire. I have suggested—and would now like to emphasize—the possibility that what is known as sexual desire may actually be quite different during these two periods. For if women prefer one or another phase, and if these preferences are accompanied by the variations in behavior which we have been discussing, what they experience as sexual desire (as well as their way of using these words) will vary accordingly. Some of the resulting confusions have already been mentioned. They also have relevance to various methods of birth control, and to the decisions that gynecologists must make in helping a woman choose a suitable form of contraception. More than one study has indicated that the rhythm method of contraception places a psychological strain upon some of the women who use it. If a woman's sexual desire normally reaches a peak during the follicular phase, she may not be able merely to *defer* it until the luteal phase. By then her particular kind of desire may have largely disappeared for that month, and in the meantime she has been forced to endure an unwelcome asceticism.

Similarly, the altering of biologically determined patterns of desire through the use of oral contraceptives may unwittingly contribute to various psychosexual problems in both male and female. Taken as a whole, the reports indicate that some women on oral contraceptives undergo an enhancement of sexual desire, while others experience the opposite. The difference among them may result from differences in the nature of their sexual desire. Women for whom sexuality means libidinal excitement of the sort that occurs more readily in the luteal phase will be satisfied with oral contraceptives, and they may even benefit in their sexual responsiveness. But for other women sexuality involves patterns of response more characteristic of the follicular phase. Their longings and their gratifications depend upon a level of estrogen which is counteracted by the progestagens in all oral contraceptives. Even if its composition favors estrogen rather than progesterone, every contraceptive pill contains enough hormones of the progesterone family to suppress the follicular phase of the cycle. Since many young women take an oral contraceptive from the very beginning of their coital activity, they can have no way of telling what their sexual preferences might have been if allowed to develop in an unaltered fashion. Through chemical intervention, their potential experience may have been weighted in favor of the sensuous. This may partly explain the great emphasis upon sensuousness which permeates our culture now more than ever. And the sensuous orientation, like the use of oral contraception, may help to save the world from the horrors of overpopulation. But the fact remains that millions of women may be sacrificing a sexuality that would have been normal and natural for them without even realizing that their lives have been changed.

To clarify these and other problems related to the nature of sexual desire, one needs subtler questionnaires than those ordinarily used. To resolve the problems about uterine suction, one needs new experimental techniques. There now exists the technological possibility of investigating sperm transport by means of pressure-sensitive radio-pills. These were used by the Foxes for measuring intrauterine pressures in the coitus of a human couple. This method has the advantage of obviating catheters and wires leading to the uterus, both of which would be a hindrance in coital experiments. It also makes it possible for investigation to occur under conditions of complete or virtual privacy. Whereas a movie camera or a tape recorder would involve some invasion of privacy, if only because human observation is thus merely deferred, tracings on a kymograph drum are too remote from sexual behavior for couples to feel that they are exhibiting themselves. The two studies of the Foxes have provided important data, but both of these studies involved only one and the same couple. Comparable evidence is needed from a much larger sample of married couples, a sample that would also include a diversity of orgasmic patterns in coitus. The subjects could use the radio-pill equipment in their own home, coitus being recorded by the couples themselves at times when it would occur spontaneously rather than at times fixed by appointment with a laboratory. If possible, multiple radio-pills should be inserted in the uterus for the sake of measuring the direction of the contractile waves.

As I have mentioned, the Foxes also recorded the occurrence of repetitive apnea just prior to a terminative orgasm in the female.[80] They did not, however, attempt to correlate the moments of intense uterine contraction with the moments of apnea, their studies on breathing patterns and intrauterine pressures having been made separately. Future research would profit by synchronizing the recording devices in such fashion as to be able to determine whether the moments of apnea—in those women who experience it—are correlated with the moments of highest intra-uterine pressure. One could thereby acquire valuable data about the relationship between respiration and orgasmic reproductive mechanisms as a whole.

If these procedures result in a clearer delineation of orgasmic patterns, questions about the optimal timing of ejaculation will need revision. What is indicated for one type of orgasm may not be indicated for another. In general, we may have to reconsider many of the current assumptions about male sexuality, both in itself and in its relationship to the female.

References

(For complete bibliographical details, cf. first listing of each work cited)

PREFACE

1. Lessing, D., *The Golden Notebook* (Harmondsworth, Middlesex, Penguin Books, 1964; first published in 1962), p. 213.
2. *Time* Magazine, November 16, 1970.

INTRODUCTION: THE NEW SEXOLOGY

1. Freud, S., *Three Essays on the Theory of Sexuality*, in *The Standard Edition of the Complete Psychological Works of Sigmund Freud*, Vol. VII (London, Hogarth Press and the Institute of Psycho-Analysis, 1957 *et seq.*). Freud's complete works are hereafter referred to as *SE*.
2. Kinsey, A. C., *et al.*, *Sexual Behavior in the Human Female* (Philadelphia, W. B. Saunders, 1953), p. 626.
3. Freud, S., *General Theory of the Neuroses*, in *SE*, Vol. XVI, p. 328.
4. *Cf.* Beach, F.A., *Hormones and Behavior* (New York, Hoeber, 1968).
5. *Cf.* Dobzhansky, T., *Mankind Evolving* (New York, Bantam Books, 1968), p. 215*ff.*
6. *Cf.* Nissen, H. W., "Social Behavior in Primates," in Stone, C.P., *Comparative Psychology* (New York, Prentice-Hall, 1951).
7. Harlow, H. F. & Harlow, M.K., "Social deprivation in monkeys," *Sci. Amer.*, 207; 136–46, 1962. *Cf.* also Harlow, H.F., "Sexual Behavior in the Rhesus Monkey," in Beach, F.A. (ed.), *Sex and Behavior* (New York, John Wiley & Sons, 1965).

8. Freud, S., *Civilization and its Discontents*, (New York, W. W. Norton, 1962), p. 52 (also in SE, Vol. XXI, p. 105).
9. Freud, S., "The Most Prevalent Form of Degradation in Erotic Life," in *Sexuality and the Psychology of Love* (New York, Collier Books, 1963), p. 68. I prefer this translation to the one in SE, Vol. XI, p. 189.
10. *Ibid.*, p. 69.
11. Masters, W. H. & Johnson, V. E., *Human Sexual Response* (Boston, Little, Brown, 1966), p. 342.
12. Kinsey, A. C., *Sexual Behavior in the Human Female*, p. 639.
13. *Ibid.*, p. 640.
14. Masters, W. H. & Johnson, V. E., *Human Sexual Response*, p. 127.
15. *Ibid.*, p. 4.
16. *Ibid.*, p. 12.
17. *Ibid.*, p. 20 and p. 8.
18. Kinsey, A. C., *Sexual Behavior in the Human Female*, p. 638.
19. Raboch, J., "Studies in the Sexuality of Women," in Gebhard, P.H., Raboch, J., Giese, H., *The Sexuality of Women* (London, André Deutsch, 1970), p. 56.
20. *Ibid.*, p. 136.

CHAPTER 1: TOWARDS SEXUAL PLURALISM

1. Ellis, A., "Is the Vaginal Orgasm a Myth?," in DeMartino, M. F. (ed.), *Sexual Behavior and Personality Characteristics* (New York, Grove Press, 1966), p. 356.
2. *Ibid.*
3. Koedt, A., "The Myth of the Vaginal Orgasm," in *Women's Liberation: Notes from the Second Year* (New York, Radical Feminism, 1970), p. 37.
4. Udry, J.R. & Morris, N.M., "Distribution of coitus in the menstrual cycle," *Nature*, 220: 593–96, 1968.
5. Sherfey, M. J., *The Nature and Evolution of Female Sexuality* (New York, Random House, 1972), pp. 142–43.
6. Masters, W. H. & Johnson, V. E., *Human Sexual Response*, pp. 135–36.
7. Pomeroy, W. B., *Girls and Sex* (Harmondsworth, Middlesex, Penguin Books, 1971), p. 75.
8. Elkan, E., "Evolution of female orgastic ability—a biological survey," *Int'nat. J. Sexology*, 2: 1–13, 84–93, 1948.

9. Kinsey, A. C, *Sexual Behavior in the Human Female*, p. 581.

10. Millett, K., *Sexual Politics* (New York, Doubleday, 1970).

11. Gebhard, P. H., "Female Sexuality," in Gebhard, P.H., Raboch, J., Giese, H., *The Sexuality of Women*, pp. 15–16.

12. Sherfey, M.J., *op. cit.*, pp. 134–35.

13. *Ibid.*, p. 135.

14. *Cf.* McDermott, S., *Studies in Female Sexuality* (London, The Odyssey Press, 1970), p. 59; Robertiello, R. C., "The 'clitoral versus vaginal orgasm' controversy and some of its ramifications," *J. Sex Research*, 6: 307–11, 1970; Fox, C. A. & Fox, B., "Blood pressure and respiratory patterns during human coitus," *J. Reprod. Fert.*, 19: 405–15, 1969; Lowen, A., *Love and Orgasm* (New York, Signet Books, 1967), p. 233ff.; Lessing, D., *The Golden Notebook*, pp. 212–13; Robinson, M. N., *The Power of Sexual Surrender* (New York, Signet Books, 1964), p. 26.

15. Robinson, M.N., *The Power of Sexual Surrender*, p. 146 and *passim*; Storr, A., *Human Aggression* (New York, Atheneum, 1968), pp. 62–63.

16. Masters, W. H. & Johnson, V.E., *Human Sexual Inadequacy* (Boston, Little, Brown, 1970).

17. Shainess, N., "Sexual inadequacy," *J. Am. Medical Ass'n.*, 213: 1970, p. 2084. *Cf.* also Shainess, N., "A Re-Assessment of Feminine Sexuality and Erotic Experience," in Masserman, J.H. (ed.), *Sexuality of Women* (New York, Grune & Stratton, 1966), p. 63.

18. Bonaparte, M., *Female Sexuality* (New York, International Universities Press, 1953); Deutsch, H., *The Psychology of Women* (London, Research Books, 1946).

19. *Ibid.*, Vol. 2, p. 74.

20. Atkinson, T., "The Institution of Sexual Intercourse," in *Women's Liberation: Notes from the Second Year* (New York, Radical Feminism, 1970).

CHAPTER 2: THE SENSUOUS AND THE PASSIONATE

1. Saint Jerome, *Against Jovinian.*

2. Quoted in Countess of Blessington, *Journal of the Conversations of Lord Byron*, 1834, p. 317.

3. Lycurgus, quoted in De Rougemont, D., *Love in the Western World* (New York, Anchor Books, 1957), p. 50.

4. Freud, S., "The Most Prevalent Form of Degradation in Erotic

Life," in *Sexuality and the Psychology of Love*, p. 67. I prefer this translation to the one in SE, Vol. XI, pp. 187–88.

5. *Ibid.*, in SE, Vol. XI, p. 180; Freud, S., "Über die allgemeinste Erniedrigung des Liebeslebens," *Beiträge zur Psychologie des Liebeslebens II, Gesammelte Schriften von Sigmund Freud, Fünfter Band* (Leipzig, Internationaler Psychoanalytischer Verlag, 1924), p. 201.

6. *Ibid.*, in SE, Vol. XI, p. 181.

7. Stendhal, *On Love* (New York, Grosset & Dunlap, 1967), p. 2.

8. *Ibid.*, p. 3.

9. *Ibid.*, p. 5.

10. Watts, A. W., *Nature, Man, and Woman* (New York, Mentor Books, 1958), p. 167.

11. Masters, W. H. & Johnson, V. E., *Human Sexual Inadequacy*, p. 309.

12. Shaw, G. B., *The Doctor's Dilemma*, Act I.

13. Reik, T., *Of Love and Lust* (New York, Farrar, Straus & Giroux, 1957), p. 190.

CHAPTER 3: TYPES OF FEMALE ORGASM

1. Levine, L., "A criterion for orgasm in the female," *Marriage Hygiene* (later *Int'nat. J. Sexology*), 1: 173–74, 1948.

2. *Ibid.*

3. Masters, W. H., quoted in Lehrman, N., *The Nature of Sex* (London, Sphere Books, 1971), p. 144.

4. Malleson, J., "A criterion for orgasm in the female," *Marriage Hygiene* (later *Int'nat. J. Sexology*), 1: 174, 1948.

5. Chesser, E., *Love and the Married Woman* (New York, G.P. Putnam's Sons, 1969), p. 190.

6. Kinsey, A. C., *Sexual Behavior in the Human Female*, p. 627.

7. *Ibid.*, p. 633.

8. *Ibid.*, p. 635.

9. Masters, W. H., quoted in "Questions and Group Discussion," appended to Masters, W. H. & Johnson, V. E., "The Sexual Response Cycles of the Human Male and Female: Comparative Anatomy and Physiology," in Beach, F.A. (ed.), *Sex and Behavior* (New York, John Wiley & Sons, 1965), p. 531.

10. Fink, P. J., "A Review of the Investigations of Masters and Johnson," in Fink, P. J. & Hammett, Van B. O. (eds.), *Sexual Function and Dysfunction* (Philadelphia, F.A. Davis, 1969), p. 9.

11. *Cf.* references in Chapter 4 of this book.

12. Quoted in Lowen, A., *Love and Orgasm*, p. 238.

13. Fox, C. A., Wolff, H. S., & Baker, J. A., "Measurement of intravaginal and intra-uterine pressures during human coitus by radiotelemetry," *J. Reprod. Fert.*, 22: 243–51, 1970; Fox, C.A. & Fox, B., "Blood pressure and respiratory patterns during human coitus," *J. Reprod. Fert.*

14. Rainwater, L., *Family Design: Marital Sexuality, Family Size, and Contraception* (Chicago, Aldine, 1965), p. 63fn.

15. Kinsey, A. C., *Sexual Behavior in the Human Female*, p. 631fn.

16. Roubaud, F., "Traité de l'impuissance et de la sterilité chez l'homme et chez la femme," 1855. Quoted in Brecher, E. M., *The Sex Researchers* (Boston, Little, Brown, 1969), pp. 288–89.

17. Quoted in Heiman, M., "Psychoanalytic Interpretations of Masters' and Johnson's Research," in Fink, P.J. & Hammett, Van B.O. (eds.), *Sexual Function and Dysfunction*, p. 43.

18. *Cf.* Fox, C.A. & Fox, B., "Blood pressure and respiratory patterns during human coitus," *J. Reprod. Fert.*

19. Robinson, M.N., *The Power of Sexual Surrender*, p. 23.

20. *Cf.* Fox, C.A. & Fox, B., "Blood pressure and respiratory patterns during human coitus," *J. Reprod. Fert.*

21. Masters, W.H., quoted in Lehrman, N., *The Nature of Sex*, p. 147.

22. Robinson, M.N., *The Power of Sexual Surrender*, p. 69.

23. Masters, W. H. & Johnson, V. E., *Human Sexual Response*, *passim*.

24. Heiman, M., "Sexual response in women," *J. Am. Psychoanalytic Ass'n*, 2: 360–85, 1963.

25. VanDemark, N.L. & Hays, R.L., "Uterine motility responses to mating," *Am. J. Physiol.*, 170: 518–21, 1952.

26. *Cf.* Fox, C.A., Wolff, H.S., & Baker, J.A., "Measurement of intravaginal and intra-uterine pressures during human coitus by radiotelemetry," *J. Reprod. Fert* ; *cf.* also Fox, C.A. & Fox, B., "Uterine suction during orgasm," *Brit. Med. J.*, 1: 300, 1967.

27. Lessing, D., *The Golden Notebook*, p. 213.

28. *Ibid.*, p. 308.

29. Masters, W. H. & Johnson, V.E., *Human Sexual Inadequacy*, p. 229 and pp. 308–9.

30. Lowen, A., *Love and Orgasm*, p. 212.

31. Kinsey, A.C. *et al.*, *Sexual Behavior in the Human Male* (Philadelphia, W.B. Saunders, 1948), p. 580.

32. Kinsey, A.C., *Sexual Behavior in the Human Female*, p. 584.

33. *Ibid.*, p. 581.

34. *Cf.* Clark, L., "Is there a difference between a clitoral and a vaginal orgasm?," *J. Sex Research*, 6: 25–28, 1970.

35. *Cf.* previous references to McDermott, S., *Studies in Female Sexuality*; Robertiello, R.C., "The 'clitoral versus vaginal orgasm' controversy and some of its ramifications," *J. Sex Research*; Fox, C. A. & Fox, B., "Blood pressure and respiratory patterns during human coitus," *J. Reprod. Fert.*; Lessing, D., *The Golden Notebook*; Lowen, A., *Love and Orgasm*; Robinson, M. N., *The Power of Sexual Surrender*.

36. Sherfey, M. J., *The Nature and Evolution of Female Sexuality*, pp. 134–35.

37. Personal communication.

38. Wallin, P. & Clark, A. L., "A study of orgasm as a condition of women's enjoyment of coitus in the middle years of marriage," *Human Biology*, 35: 131–39, 1963.

39. Quoted in Malleson, J., "Notes and comments," *Int'nat. J. Sexology*, 2: 255, 1949.

40. Masters, W. H. & Johnson, V. E., *Human Sexual Response*, p. 67.

41. Quoted in *Time* Magazine, March 20, 1972, p. 32.

42. Deutsch, H., quoted in "Panel report: frigidity in women" (B.E. Moore reporting), *J. Am. Psychoanalytic Ass'n*, 9: 571–84, 1961.

43. Malleson, J., *Any Wife or Any Husband* (Baltimore, Penguin Books, 1962), p. 97.

CHAPTER 4: THE CLITORAL-VAGINAL TRANSFER THEORY

1. Freud, S., *Three Essays on the Theory of Sexuality*, in SE, Vol. VII, p. 221.

2. *Ibid.* I have here used a preferable translation by A. A. Brill: Freud, S., *Three Contributions to the Theory of Sex* (New York and Washington, Nervous and Mental Disease Publishing Company, 1918), pp. 80–81.

3. Freud, S., *General Theory of the Neuroses*, in SE, Vol. XVI, p. 318.

4. Freud, S., *New Introductory Lectures in Psycho-Analysis*, (New York, W. W. Norton, 1965), p. 118 (also in SE, Vol. XXII, p. 118).

5. Lowen, A., *Love and Orgasm*, p. 233.

6. *Ibid.*

7. Robertiello, R.C., "The 'clitoral versus vaginal orgasm' controversy and some of its ramifications," *J. Sex Research*.

8. Payne, S.M., "A conception of femininity," *Brit. J. Med. Psychol.*, 15: 18–33, 1935.

9. Abraham, K., *Selected Papers of Karl Abraham, M.D.* (London, Hogarth Press and the Institute of Psycho-Analysis, 1948), p. 284.

10. Bergler, E. & Kroger, W.S., "The dynamic significance of vaginal lubrication to frigidity," *West. J. Surg.*, 61: 711–16, 1953.

11. Lowen, A., *op. cit.*, pp. 232–33.

12. Robinson, M.N., *The Power of Sexual Surrender*, p. 164.

13. Rado, S., "Sexual anaesthesia in the female," *Quart. Rev. Surg. Obst. & Gynec.*, 16: 249, 1959.

14. Quoted in Jones, E., *The Life and Work of Sigmund Freud* (London, Hogarth Press, 1958), Vol. II, p. 468.

15. Bonaparte, M., *Female Sexuality*, p. 121.

16. *Ibid.*, p. 138.

17. *Ibid.*, p. 111.

18. *Ibid.*, p. 85.

19. *Ibid.*, pp. 85–86.

20. *Ibid.*, p. 155.

21. *Ibid.*, p. 111.

22. *Ibid.*

23. *Ibid.*

24. *Ibid.*, p. 138.

25. *Ibid.*, p. 111.

26. O'Hare, H., "Letters to the Editor," *Int'nat. J. Sexology*, 4: 117–18, 1950; and 4: 243–44, 1951. *Cf.* also Brown, D. G. "Female Orgasm and Sexual Inadequacy," in Brecher, R. & E. (eds.), *An Analysis of Human Sexual Response* (London, Panther Books, 1968), pp. 167–68. Ellis mentions O'Hare in "Is the Vaginal Orgasm a Myth?," in DeMartino, M.F. (ed.), *Sexual Behavior and Personality Characteristics*.

27. Kinsey, A. C., *Sexual Behavior in the Human Female*, p. 584.

28. *Ibid.*, p. 580.

29. Malleson, J. "Notes and Comments," *Int'nat. J. Sexology*, 2: 255, 1949.

30. Kinsey, A.C., *Sexual Behavior in the Human Female*, p. 583.

31. *Ibid.*, pp. 581–82.

32. Clark, L., "Notes and Comments," *Int'nat. J. Sexology*, 2: 254–55, 1949.

33. Kinsey, A.C., *Sexual Behavior in the Human Female*, p. 581.

34. Masters, W.H. & Johnson, V.E., "The sexual response cycle of the

human female: III, The clitoris; anatomic and clinical considerations," *West. J. Surg.*, 70: 248–57, 1962.

35. *Ibid.*
36. Masters, W. H. & Johnson, V. E., *Human Sexual Response*, p. 66.
37. Michael, R.P. "Neuroendocrine Factors Regulating Primate Behavior," in Martini, L. & Ganong, W.F. (eds.), *Frontiers in Neuroendocrinology, 1971* (New York, Oxford University Press, 1971), p. 391.
38. Masters, W. H. & Johnson, V. E., *Human Sexual Inadequacy*, p. 304 and p. 309.
39. Clark, L., "Is there a difference between a clitoral and a vaginal orgasm?", *J. Sex Research*.
40. Personal communication.
41. *Cf.* Sigusch, V., *Exzitation und Orgasmus bei der Frau* (Stuttgart, Ferdinand Enke Verlag, 1970), pp. 51–58. *Cf.* also Hastings, D.W., *Impotence and Frigidity* (Boston, Little, Brown, 1963).
42. Malleson, J., *Any Wife or Any Husband*, p. 66.

CHAPTER 5: TWO SYSTEMS OF SEXUAL MORES

1. Kinsey, A.C., *Sexual Behavior in the Human Male*, p. 386.
2. *Ibid.*
3. *Ibid.*, p. 572.
4. *Ibid.*
5. *Ibid.*
6. *Ibid.*, p. 385.
7. *Ibid.*
8. Masters, W. H. & Johnson, V. E., *Human Sexual Response*, p. 12.
9. *Ibid.*, p. 14.
10. *Ibid.*, p. 12.
11. Kinsey, A.C., *Sexual Behavior in the Human Male*, p. 386.
12. *Ibid.*, p. 389.
13. Clark, L., "The Range and Variety of Questions People Ask about Sex," in Vincent, C. E. (ed.), *Human Sexuality in Medical Education and Practice* (Springfield, Illinois, C. C. Thomas, 1968), p. 561.
14. Mead, M., "Cultural Determinants of Behavior," in Young, W. C. & Corner, G. W. (eds.), *Sex and Internal Secretions* (Baltimore, Williams & Wilkins, 1961), Vol. 2, p. 1434.
15. Farber, L. H., *The Ways of the Will* (London, Constable, 1966), p. 71.

16. Quoted in Lehrman, N., *The Nature of Sex*, p. 143.
17. *Ibid.*
18. Quoted in Brecher, E. M., *The Sex Researchers*, p. 196.
19. Robinson, M. N., *The Power of Sexual Surrender*, p. 24.
20. Kinsey, A. C., *Sexual Behavior in the Human Male*, pp. 577–78.
21. Bergler, E., *Counterfeit Sex: Homosexuality, Impotence, Frigidity* (New York, Evergreen Black Cat, 1961), p. 282.
22. Quoted in Wong, A., "Traditional Chinese attitude to sex and woman," *Marriage Hygiene* (later *Int'nat. J. Sexology*), 1: 151–55, 1948.
23. Reich, W., *The Function of the Orgasm* (London, Panther Books, 1968), p. 350; Masters, W. H. & Johnson, V. E., *Human Sexual Inadequacy*, p. 303. *Cf.* also Pellegrino, V., "New Love Techniques We Learned at the Masters and Johnson Sex Clinic," in Robbins, J. & J. (eds.), *An Analysis of Human Sexual Inadequacy* (New York, Signet Books, 1970).
24. "J," *The Sensuous Woman* (New York, Lyle Stuart, 1969), p. 113.
25. Mudd, E.H., in "Roundtable: Frigidity" (J.P. Brady, moderator), *Med. Asp. Hum. Sexuality*, 2 (2): 26–32, 1968.
26. Masters, W. H. & Johnson, V. E., *Human Sexual Inadequacy*, p. 310 and p. 111.
27. Beigel, H. G., "The meaning of coital postures," *Int'nat. J. Sexology*, 6: 136–43, 1953; reprinted in DeMartino, M.F. (ed.), *Sexual Behavior and Personality Characteristics*.
28. Elkan, E., "Evolution of female orgastic ability—a biological survey," *Int'nat. J. Sexology*.
29. Masters, W. H. & Johnson, V. E., *Human Sexual Inadequacy*, p. 315.
30. Quoted in Elkan, E., *op. cit.*
31. Lazarus, A. A., in "Roundtable: Frigidity" (J.P. Brady, moderator), *Med. Asp. Hum. Sexuality*, 2 (2): 26–32, 1968.

CHAPTER 6: VARIATIONS IN THE MALE

1. *Cf.* Reich, W., *The Function of the Orgasm; cf.* also Lowen, A., *Love and Orgasm*.
2. Kinsey, A. C., *Sexual Behavior in the Human Male*, p. 159.
3. *Ibid.*
4. Masters, W. H. & Johnson, V. E., *Human Sexual Response*.
5. Lowen, A., *op. cit.*, p. 228.
6. Kinsey, A. C., *Sexual Behavior in the Human Male*, pp. 160–61.

7. Lowen, A., *op. cit.*, p. 229.

8. Robinson, M. N., *The Power of Sexual Surrender*, pp. 157–58.

9. Lowen, A., *op. cit.*, p. 226.

10. *Ibid.*, p. 227.

11. *Ibid.*, p. 229.

12. Reich, W., *op. cit.*, p. 114.

13. *Ibid.*, p. 370.

14. Masters, W. H. & Johnson, V. E., *Human Sexual Response*, p. 216.

15. Lowen, A., *op. cit.*, p. 181.

16. *Ibid.*

17. Masters, W. H. & Johnson, V. E., *Human Sexual Inadequacy*, p. 323.

18. Reich, W., *op. cit.*, pp. 114–19.

19. Reik, T., "Quotations from Theodor Reik," *Med. Asp. Hum. Sexuality*, 5 (1): 195, 1971.

20. Kinsey, A. C., *Sexual Behavior in the Human Male*, p. 580.

21. Hohmann, G. W., "Some effects of spinal cord lesions on experienced emotional feelings," *Psychophysiology*, 3: 143–56, 1966. *Cf.* also Money, J., "Sex Hormones and Other Variables in Human Eroticism," in Young, W. C. & Corner, G. W. (eds.), *Sex and Internal Secretions* (Baltimore, Williams & Wilkins, 1961), Vol. 2.

22. Fox, C. A., Ismail, A. A. A., Love, D. N., Kirkham, K. E., & Loraine, J. A., "Studies on the relationship between plasma testosterone levels and human sexual activity," *J. Endocr.*, 52, 1972.

23. Katongole, C. B., Naftolin, F., & Short, R. V., "Relationship between blood levels and luteinizing hormone and testosterone in bulls, and the effects of sexual stimulation," *J. Endocr.*, 50: 457–66, 1971.

24. *Cf.* Michael, R. P. & Keverne, E. B., "Primate sex pheromones of vaginal origin," *Nature* (London), 225: 84–85, 1970.

25. *Cf.* Davenport, W., "Sexual Patterns and Their Regulation in a Society of the Southwest Pacific," in Beach, F.A. (ed.), *Sex and Behavior* (New York, John Wiley & Sons, 1965), pp. 183–84.

26. Freud, S., *Civilization and its Discontents*, (New York, W. W. Norton), p. 52 (also in SE, Vol. XXI, p. 105).

27. De Beauvoir, S., *The Second Sex* (New York, Bantam Books, 1961).

28. Carr, D.E., *The Sexes* (New York, Doubleday, 1970), pp. 96–97.

29. Lessing, D., *The Golden Notebook*, pp. 212–13.

30. Masters, W. H. & Johnson, V. E., *Human Sexual Inadequacy*, p. 241.

31. Deutsch, H., *The Psychology of Women*, Vol. 2, p. 78.
32. Lowen, A., *op. cit.*, p. 172.
33. Reich, W., *op. cit.*, p. 170.
34. Lewis, L.S. & Brissett, D., "Sex as work: a study of avocational counseling," *Social Problems*, 15, 8, 1967; cited in Taylor, L., "The unfinished sexual revolution," *J. Biosoc. Sci.*, 3: 473–92, 1971.
35. Masters, W.H. & Johnson, V.E., *Human Sexual Inadequacy*, p. 92.

CONCLUSION: THE LIMITATIONS OF PLURALISM

1. Sherfey, M.J., *The Nature and Evolution of Female Sexuality*, p. 110.
2. *Ibid.*, pp. 112–13.
3. Freud, S., " 'Civilized' Sexual Morality and Modern Nervous Illness," in *SE*, Vol. IX.
4. Quoted in Jones, E., *The Life and Work of Sigmund Freud*, Vol. III, pp. 208–9.

APPENDIX: FERTILITY AND THE FEMALE ORGASM

1. *Cf.* De Ropp, R.S., *Sex Energy* (New York, Dell, 1970).
2. Masters, W.H. & Johnson, V. E., *Human Sexual Response*, p. 124.
3. *Ibid.*, p. 122.
4. *Ibid.*, p. 116.
5. Fox, C.A. & Fox, B., "Uterine suction during orgasm," *Brit. Med. J.*
6. Masters, W.H. & Johnson, V. E., *Human Sexual Response*, p. 116.
7. *Ibid.*, p. 118.
8. Hartman, C.G. & Ball, J., "On the almost instantaneous transport of spermatozoa through the cervix and the uterus of the rat," *Proc. Soc. exp Biol. Med.*, 28: 312–14, 1930.
9. VanDemark, N.L. & Moeller, A. N., "Speed of spermatozoan transport in reproductive tract of estrous cow," *Am. J. Physiol.*, 165: 674–79, 1951.
10. Evans, E.I., "The transport of spermatozoa in the dog," *Am. J. Physiol.*, 105: 287–93, 1933.
11. Ford, C.S. & Beach, F.A., *Patterns of Sexual Behavior* (New York, Ace Books, 1951), p. 48.
12. *Ibid.*, p. 41.
13. *Cf.* Schaller, G.B., *The Mountain Gorilla: Ecology and Behavior*

(Chicago, U. of Chicago Press, 1963). Orangutan: personal communication from Rodman, J.C.

14. Kinsey, A.C., *Sexual Behavior in the Human Female*, p. 629.

15. Cf. Sobrero, A.J., "Sperm Migration in the Human Female," in Westin, B. & Wiqvist, N. (eds.), *Fertility and Sterility: Proceedings of Fifth World Congress* (Amsterdam, Excerpta Medica Publishers, 1967), p. 701.

16. Egli, G.E. & Newton, M., "The transport of carbon particles in the human female reproductive tract," *Fert. Steril.*, 12: 151–55, 1961.

17. Cf. Csapo, A., "The diagnostic significance of the intrauterine pressure," *Obst. & Gynec. Survey*, 25: 403–35; 515–43, 1970.

18. Lightfoot, R.J. & Restall, B.J., "Effects of site of insemination, sperm motility and genital tract contractions on transport of spermatozoa in the ewe," *J. Reprod. Fert.*, 26: 1–13, 1971.

19. Fox, C.A., Wolff, H.S., & Baker, J.A., "Measurement of intravaginal and intra-uterine pressures during human coitus by radiotelemetry," *J. Reprod. Fert.*

20. Masters, W.H. & Johnson, V.E., *Human Sexual Response*, p. 117.

21. Reich, W., *The Function of the Orgasm*, p. 315.

22. Masters, W.H. & Johnson, V.E., *Human Sexual Response*, p. 118.

23. Cf. Von Euler, U. S. & Eliasson, R., *Prostaglandins* (New York, Academic Press, 1967), p. 62.

24. De Carteret, R. J., "Uterine suction during orgasm," *Brit. Med. J.*, 1967: (1): 761, 1967.

25. Cf. Ramwell, P. W., Shaw, J. E., Kucharski, J., "Prostaglandin: release from the rat phrenic nerve-diaphragm preparation," *Science*, 149: 1390–91, 1965.

26. Masters, W. H. & Johnson, V. E., *Human Sexual Response*, p. 194.

27. *Ibid.*, p. 114.

28. Kinsey, A. C., *Sexual Behavior in the Human Female*, p. 584.

29. Cf. Robinson, M. N., *The Power of Sexual Surrender*, p. 22.

30. Bonaparte, M., *Female Sexuality*, p. 85; Masters, W. H. & Johnson, V. E., *Human Sexual Response*, p. 194.

31. *Ibid.*, p. 113.

32. Hartman, C. G., "How do sperms get into the uterus?", *Fert. Steril.*, 8: 403–27, 1957.

33. Belonoschkin, B., *Zeugung beim Menschen im Lichter der Spermatozoenlehre* (Stockholm, Sjoberg Forlag, 1949).

34. Quoted in Hartman, C.G., "How do sperms get into the uterus?", *Fert. Steril.*

35. Sobrero, A. J., "Sperm Migration in the Human Female," in Westin, B. & Wiqvist, N. (eds.), *Fertility and Sterility: Proceedings of Fifth World Congress.*

36. Fox, C. A. & Fox, B., "A comparative study of coital physiology, with special reference to the sexual climax," *J. Reprod. Fert.*, 24: 319–36, 1971.

37. Fox, C. A. & Fox, B., "Blood pressure and respiratory patterns during human coitus," *J. Reprod. Fert.*

38. Zumpe, D. & Michael, R. P., "The clutching reaction and orgasm in the female rhesus monkey (*M. mulatta*)," *J. Endocr.*, 40: 117–23, 1968.

39. Reik, T., *Of Love and Lust*, p. 419.

40. Zumpe, D. & Michael, R. P., *op. cit.*

41. Kinsey, A. C., *Sexual Behavior in the Human Male*, p. 580.

42. *Ibid.*

43. *Cf.* Kleegman, S. J., "Clinical Applications of Masters' and Johnson's Research," in Fink, P. J. & Hammett, Van B. O. (eds.), *Sexual Function and Dysfunction.*

44. Masters, W. H. & Johnson, V. E., *Human Sexual Inadequacy*, *passim.*

45. Malinowski, B., *The Sexual Life of Savages* (New York, Halcyon House, 1929).

46. Cavanagh, J. R., "Rhythm of sexual desire in women," *Med. Asp. Hum. Sexuality*, 3: (2): 29–39, 1969.

47. James, W. H., "The distribution of coitus within the human intermenstruum," *J. Biosoc. Sci.*, 3: 159–71, 1971.

48. Tinklepaugh, O. L., "The nature of periods of sex desire in woman and their relation to ovulation," *Am J. Obst. & Gynec.*, 26: 335–45, 1933.

49. *Ibid.*

50. Money, J., "Influence of hormones on sexual behavior," *Annual Rev. Med.*, 16: 67–82, 1965.

51. Money, J., "Influence of hormones on psychosexual differentiation," *Med. Asp. Hum. Sexuality*, 2: 1968.

52. Sherfey, M. J., *The Nature and Evolution of Female Sexuality*, p. 96.

53. Kinsey, A. C., *Sexual Behavior in the Human Female*, p. 610.

54. *Ibid.*, p. 608.

55. Hartman, C. G., *Science and the Safe Period* (London, Baillière, Tindall, & Cox, 1962), p. 155.

56. Masters, W. H., "The Sexual Response Cycle of the Human Fe-

male: Vaginal Lubrication," in *Annals of the New York Academy of Sciences*, 83: 301–17, 1959.

57. Sherfey, M. J., *op. cit.*, p. 97.

58. *Ibid.*, p. 113.

59. Michael, R. P., "Neuroendocrine Factors Regulating Primate Behavior," in Martini, L. & Ganong, W. F. (eds.), *Frontiers in Neuroendocrinology*, 1971.

60. Davis, K. B., *Factors in the Sex Life of 2200 Women* (New York, Harper, 1929); Hart, R. D'A., "Monthly rhythm of libido in married women," *Brit. Med. J.*, 1960 (1): 1023–24, 1960.

61. Cavanagh, J. R., *op. cit.*

62. *Ibid.*

63. *Ibid.*

64. Stopes, M., *Married Love* (London, Hogarth Press, 1918).

65. Dickinson, R. L., "The 'safe period' as a birth control measure," *Am. J. Obst. & Gynec.*, 14: 718–30, 1927.

66. *Ibid.*

67. Cf. Hartman, C. G., *Science and the Safe Period*, pp. 73–74.

68. McCance, R. A., Luff, M. C., & Widdowson, E. E., "Physical and emotional periodicity in women," *J. Hyg.*, 37: 571–611, 1937.

69. Hartman, C. G. & Leathem, J. H., "Oogenesis and Ovulation," in Hartman, C. G. (ed.), *Mechanisms Concerned with Conception* (New York, Pergamon Press, 1963).

70. Hartman, C. G., *Science and the Safe Period*, p. 194.

71. Clark, J. H. & Zarrow, M. X., "Influence of copulation on time of ovulation in women," *Am. J. Obst. & Gynec.*, 109: 1083–85, 1971.

72. Linzenmeier, G., "Zur Frage der Empfängniszeit der Frau: Hat Knaus oder Stieve recht?", *Zentralblatt für Gynäkologie*, 69: 1108–11, 1947; statistics presented in Jöchle, W., "Coitus induced ovulation" (unpublished paper).

73. Bickenbach, W., Döring, G. K., & Hossfeld, C., "Experimentelle Frühovulation durch Cervixreizung beim Menschen," *Archiv für Gynäkologie*, 192: 412–19, 1960.

74. Aron, C., Asch, G., & Roos, J., "Triggering of ovulation by coitus in the rat," *Int'nat'l Rev. Cytol.*, 20: 139–72, 1966.

75. Zarrow, M. X. & Clark, J. H., "Ovulation following vaginal stimulation in a spontaneous ovulator and its implications," *J. Endocr.*, 40: 343–52, 1968.

76. Clark, J. H. & Zarrow, M. X., "Influence of copulation on time of ovulation in women," *Am. J. Obst. & Gynec.*

77. Zarrow, M. X. & Clark, J. H., "Ovulation following vaginal stimu-

lation in a spontaneous ovulator and its implications," *J. Endocr.*

78. Clark, J. H. & Zarrow, M. X., "Influence of copulation on time of ovulation in women," *Am. J. Obst. & Gynec.*

79. Hartman, C. G., *Science and the Safe Period*, p. 221. *Cf.* also Hartman, C. G. & Leathem, J. H., "Oogenesis and Ovulation," in Hartman, C. G. (ed.), *Mechanisms Concerned with Conception.*

80. Fox, C. A. & Fox, B., "Blood pressure and respiratory patterns during human coitus," *J. Reprod. Fert.*

Index